Wee Book of
AYE or NAW?

Wee Book of
AYE or NAW?

CAT HARVEY

Illustrations by
JESSICA HARVEY

BLACK & WHITE PUBLISHING

First published in the UK in 2023 by
Black & White Publishing Ltd
Nautical House, 104 Commercial Street, Edinburgh, EH6 6NF

A division of Bonnier Books UK
4th Floor, Victoria House, Bloomsbury Square, London, WC1B 4DA
Owned by Bonnier Books
Sveavägen 56, Stockholm, Sweden

The publisher has made every reasonable effort to contact copyright holders
of images in the picture section. Any errors are inadvertent and anyone who
for any reason has not been contacted is invited to write to the publisher so
that a full acknowledgement can be made in subsequent editions of this work.

Cat Harvey has assigned 100% of her author royalties from sales of this book to
Cash For Kids to support disadvantaged children across Scotland, equivalent to
10% of cash received by the publisher from sales. The remaining percentage
covers production, sales, distribution and publisher costs.

Use of the Cash for Kids logo is by kind permission of Bauer Media's
Cash for Kids, registered charity 1122062, SC041421 and SC003334.

A CIP catalogue record for this book is available from the British Library.

ISBN: 978 1 78530 532 0

3 5 7 9 10 8 6 4 2

Typeset by Iolaire Typesetting
Printed and bound in Great Britain by Clays Ltd, Elcograf S.p.A.

www.blackandwhitepublishing.com

For Denise Murray

My wonderful friend for 35 years, taken far too soon. Thank you for the Partick Thistle and Scotland adventures, the laughs and all the happy memories.

For always being up for nonsense and for being a wonderful mum to your three beautiful children, Cameron, Heather and Kirsty. To Duncan, Irene and Janis Murray, I'm with you all the way.

Denise, we will all miss you every day, even if you did have a weird obsession for Korean boybands. Fly high, my friend. Hopefully Scotland or Thistle will win something one day. We live in hope. We always do . . .

'*She's Electric – she's got a family full of eccentrics!*'

– OASIS

'*The seaweed is always greener in somebody else's lake, you dream about going up there but that's just a big mistake.*'

– Sebastian the Crab
The Little Mermaid

A Note From the Author

Once again here is my official disclaimer. Whilst Greatest Hits Radio and Cash for Kids will support this book, the nonsense within is completely of my own doing. Any mistakes or naughty bits are mine and mine alone. They are good professional people.

I am shifty at best.

Cat xx

CONTENTS

Foreword From
Cash for Kids

On behalf of everyone at Cash for Kids, I would like to wish Cat success with her new book. Cat has always been the most amazing ambassador for Cash for Kids in Scotland. We fundraise all year and grant the funds throughout the year to help children and young people who are disadvantaged.

Everything raised in a local area stays in that local area, so people can feel confident they are helping the children of Scotland and close to the area that matters to them.

At Cash for Kids, we support children and young people affected by poverty, abuse, neglect and life-limiting illnesses, and those who have additional needs.

One of our key priority areas is holiday hunger – for many children, school holidays are no holiday at all, they can be a living nightmare being away from the support of school, and many will be at increased risk of neglect and abuse.

In addition, with the current cost of living crisis, many families are having to make difficult choices daily, like whether to 'heat their home or eat'. Many of the families we support are working families, for whom Cash for Kids has become a lifeline.

Cat's previous book, *Cat's Out the Bag,* raised over £100,000 for Cash for Kids, allowing us to support many children and young people across Scotland with a Cost-of-Living Grant. We are delighted that Cat has chosen to support us once again with her new book.

Thank you, Cat, for your continued generosity.

Grace Reilly
Regional Charity Manager
Cash for Kids

A Wee Peek Inside My Head

by Ewen Cameron

Do I enjoy playing Aye or Naw? Aye!
　Does it do my nut in? Aye!
　Do I learn new things from Aye or Naw? Aye!
　Do people laugh at my reasoning? Aye!
　Does Aye or Naw make me feel even more of a fud? Aye!

It's a game that you'll love, hate and be amazed by. Every morning we know that workplaces across the country religiously tune in and debate the question before Cat reveals the answer.

I also know of many listeners who have placed bets on what the answer is and whoever lost buys lunch. I have lost many a bet and I think I owe Producer Cat at least fifteen McDonald's breakfasts.

I've had way too many meltdowns playing the game live on the radio because Cat is very good at asking questions that can confuse if you don't listen to the way the question is structured.

My advice is:

> Use your ears.
> Listen very carefully.
> Deconstruct the question.
> Don't rush your answer.
> Trust your gut.

After doing all this there's still a very good chance you'll be wrong, and you can then join me in 'Fud Club' where I reside as King. There are two rules of 'Fud Club':

> RULE 1 – You DON'T talk about 'Fud Club'
> RULE 2 – You DON'T EVER talk about 'Fud Club'

There is nothing to be ashamed of should you join me in this exclusive club, and to be honest it's kind of lonely being the only member in this institution, so I'm looking forward to welcoming many of you to my team.

And finally, I'm going to leave you with a question: if a pig loses its voice, is it disgruntled? . . . AYE or NAW?

Enjoy, my friends.

Love, EWEN

Introduction

Hello and welcome to *Ewen and Cat's Wee Book of Aye or Naw?* I mean we all know it's really '*Cat's Wee Book of Aye or Naw?*' because I've spent eight months working on it and he did he-haw and then rocked up for a photo, but we are a team. Through thick and thin. So, I'll let him share the joy!

This is a little book packed full of questions that will amuse, inform and probably infuriate you in equal measure. I hope you have as much fun enjoying these as I've had tormenting Ewen Cameron, my radio co-host, with them over the past few years.

It is the perfect book to play with friends, to read in the loo, or to give as a Secret Santa present as it's under a tenner and ALL the royalties go to Cash for Kids. You'll learn five hundred fun but ultimately useless facts and do a good thing at the same time. Win-win!

First, let me answer a few questions:

Can you play it competitively?

AYE. Play against a pal or form teams. First to guess 3, 5, 10, 100 etc. correctly wins. You can choose your own number depending on how much time you have. (Adults could add a drinking game element if they fancied. Losing team downs a shot. Although I would suggest this would work best after you've completed your chosen length of game, not per question, or you'll end up spangled within a couple of pages.)

Are there clues?

AYE. For each question, I have given you Ewen's answer on the day, kind of like your 50/50 choice on *Who Wants to Be a Millionaire?*, although please remember it's EWEN and quite frankly he's an eejit. I have also given the results of the daily Twitter poll (yes I know it is now called X but nobody will ever call it that!), I guess this is like the 'ask the audience' option on the TV show. Remember, the highest percentage may not always be correct. Use these as a guide or ignore them, your choice.

Is there a carefully constructed thematic journey?

NAW. The questions appear in the random order I asked them on our radio show since the feature began in January 2021.

I came up with the concept of 'Aye or Naw?' just before I re-joined Ewen full-time on the breakfast show. When I say I came up with it, I'm maybe blowing my own kazoo a bit too much as it is hardly an original idea. It's basically a true or false question or a 50/50 question. You are either right or you are wrong.

However, I wanted everyone to know we are Scottish, on a Scottish show, broadcasting all over Scotland, so there was my inspired tweak. The unique selling point – the name. Yes or no, true or false became 'Aye or Naw' and it stuck.

I still have it written on my white board at home – 'AYE or NAW'. Next to a wheely bin timetable, a feature idea called 'What to Do With Old Shoes', which funnily enough hasn't made it to air yet and a Post-it reminder to phone the plumber. I am sure Ken Bruce was the same with the development of *PopMaster*. (More on my new radio bestie later.)

The best part of this little segment on our show is how seriously Ewen takes it and how often he gets it wrong. His theories are as outrageous as they are funny.

I love how people get in touch from all over the country telling us they're playing along at their school, work, bus, train, office, café, factory, canteen or building site. Kudos is not the only thing available for trouncing your work mates, some people have much higher stakes. Like Kevin and David in their painters' van, they decide who buys lunch on a daily basis depending on who gets the right answer.

NOW THIS IS IMPORTANT: all answers were correct at the time of broadcast. That's why I have added the date to when the question was first asked. (Well, they were as correct as Google told me they were, some answers may change over time.)

I find my questions in various ways. They could be topical, like a big football game, concert, or National Day, they now have one of these for nearly everything.

It could be on a whim. It could simply be a word or subject

I've just thought about. Or it could be about animals, music, science, history or geography for no other reason than I don't think there's been a question about these subjects for a while. Mostly though, they are truly random.

It will come as no surprise to reveal that I'm NOT an expert on the population of Ecuador, the scientific properties of pineapples or the density and chemical breakdown of animal farts, but I am a keen learner of new fun facts. I do check at least two or three different sources to establish the right answer. But if any answers in this book are wrong then I'm sorry. I tried, really, I did! I blame the internet and . . . oh jeezo get a life, it is a charity book for a bit of fun and not a definitive study guide for *University Challenge*!

As an added bonus, I have decided to fling in a spattering of fun stories and photos from *Ewen and Cat at Breakfast*, along the way. These should hopefully put a smile on your face, but they'll also serve as a helpful reminder to myself when I'm old and doddery of the fun and nonsense I called work back in the day.

Thank you so much for listening to our show, thank you from the bottom of my heart for buying this book and thank you for helping Cash for Kids continue to help children and families dealing with poverty throughout Scotland.

Now shall we get started? AYE . . .

Did I Steal Marti's Tunnock's Teacake?

Aye or Naw?

Marti Pellow was my first love. The Wet Wet Wet album *Popped In Souled Out* came out when I was at school and had just starting to realise boys existed.

Ewen loves to wind me up, as I still go all giggly, girly, and gushy when I see Marti, and we've seen him a lot recently. Ewen brought him into the studio as a surprise for me when my last book was just released. I never knew he was coming and basically nearly keeled over. I'm not a hugger but I squealed and ran to squash him with a bear hug.

Since then, he has been in a few times, always full of banter and always looking and smelling magnificent. He invited us to join him in his dressing room backstage at the Usher Hall in Edinburgh after his solo show. His dressing room was full of fruit, herbal teas, water and healthy stuff, but despite this we had a great time. ☺

Fast forward a year and he invited us backstage again at the Armadillo after the incredible concert accompanied by a full orchestra replaying all of *Popped In Souled Out* live. Again, he was surrounded by healthy stuff – apples, celery, ginger, herbal teas – and then I spotted it. A plate of Tunnock's teacakes.

I'm not much of a thief; a few flumps from a Woolworths pick 'n' mix when I was about six as a dare, had previously been it. I lived with fear for weeks after that and decided a life of crime was not for me. But I needed that teacake. Marti's teacake.

So, when everyone else was chatting, I slipped it in my pocket. I know he would have given me it if I asked, so I don't know why I did it. Kind of like stealing his pants, I guess, but tastier.

I still have it in my house. Like a weird sugary trophy. Marti's teacake. I show it to friends. They tell me I'm a weirdo. It shall live in my cupboard until someone eats it by mistake.

Until then it will remain just like its original owner – TEMPTATION!

So, did I steal Marti's Tunnock's Teacake? Shamefully the answer to this one is AYE!

Jan – March 2021

QUESTION 1
11.1.21

The Sultan of Brunei once spent over £20,000 importing Irn-Bru for a Burns Supper. Is this true? Aye or Naw?

Ewen Says: Naw
Twitter Says: Aye 81%; Naw 19%
You Say: **Aye** or **Naw**?

QUESTION 2
12.1.21

The shortest street in the world is in Scotland.
Is this true? Aye or Naw?

Ewen Says: Naw
Twitter Says: Aye 70%; Naw 30%
You Say: **Aye** or **Naw**?

QUESTION 3
13.1.21

Hollywood star Gerry Butler trained as an accountant before becoming an actor. Is this true? Aye or Naw?

Ewen Says: Aye
Twitter Says: Aye 71%; Naw 29%
You Say: **Aye** or **Naw**?

QUESTION 4
14.1.21

Queen Victoria smoked cigarettes on her trips to Scotland to get rid of midges. Is this true? Aye or Naw?

Ewen Says: Aye
Twitter Says: Aye 83% ; Naw 17%
You Say: **Aye** or **Naw**?

QUESTION 5
15.1.21

The Scottish Classic 'Ye Canny Shove Yer Grannie Aff a Bus' is based on a nineteenth century Finnish folk song where you were encouraged NOT to throw your grandmother off a sleigh. Is this true? Aye or Naw?

Ewen Says: Naw
Twitter Says: Aye 42%; Naw 58%
You Say: **Aye** or **Naw**?

QUESTION 6
18.1.21 – Blue Monday – the most depressing day of the year.

New Order's smash hit 'Blue Monday' was in the singles charts for over 150 weeks. Is this true? Aye or Naw?

Ewen Says: Naw
Twitter Says: Aye 70%; Naw 30%
You Say: **Aye** or **Naw?**

QUESTION 7
19.1.21

The Scotland men's football team have qualified for nine world cups. Is this true? Aye or Naw?

Ewen Says: Naw
Twitter Says: Aye 31%; Naw 69%
You Say: **Aye** or **Naw?**

QUESTION 8
20.1.21 – Penguin Awareness Day

A penguin at Edinburgh Zoo holds a very high rank in the Norwegian Army. Is this true? Aye or Naw?

Ewen Says: Aye
Twitter Says: Aye 81%; Naw 29%
You Say: **Aye** or **Naw?**

QUESTION 9
21.1.21

The magician who made famous the trick of pulling a white rabbit from a top hat was from Aberdeen. Is this true? Aye or Naw?

Ewen Says: Naw
Twitter Says: Aye 19%; Naw 81%
You Say: **Aye** or **Naw?**

QUESTION 10
22.1.21

Hollywood star Bill Murray once gate-crashed a student party in St Andrews, did the dishes in the sink then left. Is this true? Aye or Naw?

Ewen Says: Aye
Twitter Says: Aye 54%; Naw 46%
You Say: **Aye** or **Naw?**

QUESTION 11
25.1.21 – Burns Night

Michael Jackson's song 'Thriller' was inspired by Robert Burns' poem 'Tam o' Shanter'. Is this true? Aye or Naw?

Ewen Says: Naw
Twitter Says: Aye 12%; Naw 88%
You Say: **Aye** or **Naw?**

QUESTION 12
26.1.21 – Australia Day

The Australian National Anthem was written by
a Scotsman. Is this true? Aye or Naw?

Ewen Says: Aye
Twitter Says: Aye 50%; Naw 50%
You Say: **Aye** or **Naw?**

QUESTION 13
1.2.21

Chicken Tikka Masala was invented in Glasgow.
Is this true? Aye or Naw?

Ewen Says: Naw
Twitter Says: Aye 40%; Naw 60%
You Say: **Aye** or **Naw**?

QUESTION 14
2.2.21

The River Clyde is the longest river in Scotland.
Is this true? Aye or Naw?

Ewen Says: Naw
Twitter Says: Aye 39%; Naw 61%
You Say: **Aye** or **Naw**?

QUESTION 15
3.2.21

Dundee was the first city in the world to have its own fire brigade. Is this true? Aye or Naw?

Ewen Says: Naw
Twitter Says: Aye 37%; Naw 63%
You Say: **Aye** or **Naw**?

QUESTION 16
4.2.21

The Perthshire town of Dull is twinned with Boring in America and Bland in Australia. Is this true? Aye or Naw?

Ewen Says: Naw
Twitter Says: Aye 57%; Naw 43%
You Say: **Aye** or **Naw**?

QUESTION 17
5.2.21

The sport of ice skating began in Scotland. Is this true? Aye or Naw?

Ewen Says: Naw
Twitter Says: Aye 30%; Naw 70%
You Say: **Aye** or **Naw**?

QUESTION 18
8.2.21

The coastline of Scotland is three times longer than the coastline of England. Is this true? Aye or Naw?

Ewen Says: Aye
Twitter Says: Aye 55%; Naw 45%
You Say: **Aye** or **Naw**?

QUESTION 19
9.2.21

There's an old Scottish law stating a Scotsman who IS wearing underwear under his kilt can be fined two cans of beer. Is this true? Aye or Naw?

Ewen Says: Naw
Twitter Says: Aye 24%; Naw 76%
You Say: **Aye** or **Naw**?

QUESTION 20
10.2.21

Loch Lomond holds more fresh water than all the lochs and lakes in England and Wales combined. Is this true? Aye or Naw?

Ewen Says: Naw
Twitter Says: Aye 37%; Naw 63%
You Say: **Aye** or **Naw**?

QUESTION 21
11.2.21

The famous 1980s arcade game Pac-Man was invented in Dundee. Is this true? Aye or Naw?

Ewen Says: Naw
Twitter Says: Aye 40%; Naw 60%
You Say: **Aye** or **Naw**?

QUESTION 22
12.2.21

Glasgow should be one of the most romantic cities in the world, because the remains of St Valentine rest here. Is this true? Aye or Naw?

Ewen Says: Aye
Twitter Says: Aye 62%; Naw 38%
You Say: **Aye** or **Naw**?

QUESTION 23
15.2.21

There are more than thirty places in the world called Aberdeen. Is this true? Aye or Naw?

Ewen Says: Naw
Twitter Says: Aye 23%; Naw 77%
You Say: **Aye** or **Naw**?

QUESTION 24
16.2.21

Former Scotland manager Berti Vogts once owned a llama. Is this true? Aye or Naw?

Ewen Says: Aye
Twitter Says: Aye 49%; Naw 51%
You Say: **Aye** or **Naw**?

QUESTION 25
17.2.21

Clapshot is a traditional Scottish dish made from mashed potato and turnip. Is this true? Aye or Naw?

Ewen Says: Naw
Twitter Says: Aye 40%; Naw 60%
You Say: **Aye** or **Naw**?

QUESTION 26
18.2.21

Scottish singer Lulu was born in Newcastle before her family moved to Dennistoun when she was a baby. Is this true? Aye or Naw?

Ewen Says: Naw
Twitter Says: Aye 38%; Naw 62%
You Say: **Aye** or **Naw**?

QUESTION 27
19.2.21

The name Kirkcaldy means cold church in Gaelic.
Is this true? Aye or Naw?

Ewen Says: Aye
Twitter Says: Aye 52%; Naw 48%
You Say: **Aye** or **Naw**?

QUESTION 28
22.2.21

The waterproof raincoat was invented by a scientist
from Scotland. Is this true? Aye or Naw?

Ewen Says: Aye
Twitter Says: Aye 83%; Naw17%
You Say: **Aye** or **Naw**?

QUESTION 29
23.2.21

Richard and Maurice McDonald, the brothers who
founded the McDonald's fast food chain, are half Scottish,
as their mum was from Caithness. Is this true? Aye or Naw?

Ewen Says: Aye
Twitter Says: Aye 59%; Naw 41%
You Say: **Aye** or **Naw**?

QUESTION 30
24.2.21

A tattie-bogle is a Scottish name for a scarecrow.
Is this true? Aye or Naw?

Ewen Says: Naw
Twitter Says: Aye 57%; Naw 43%
You Say: **Aye** or **Naw**?

QUESTION 31
25.2.21

Jenners in Edinburgh once sold haggis flavoured
jellybeans. Is this true? Aye or Naw?

Ewen Says: Aye
Twitter Says: Aye 71%; Naw 29%
You Say: **Aye** or **Naw**?

QUESTION 32
26.2.21

Edinburgh Zoo was once home to a baby pterodactyl.
Is this true? Aye or Naw?

Ewen Says: Naw
Twitter Says: Aye 28%; Naw 82%
You Say: **Aye** or **Naw**?

QUESTION 33
1.3.21

The oldest Post Office in the world is in Dumfries and Galloway. Is this true? Aye or Naw?

Ewen Says: Naw
Twitter Says: Aye 52%; Naw 48%
You Say: **Aye** or **Naw?**

QUESTION 34
2.3.21

Welly boots were invented in Greenock.
Is this true? Aye or Naw?

Ewen Says: Naw
Twitter Says: Aye 61%; Naw 39%
You Say: **Aye** or **Naw?**

QUESTION 35
3.3.21

The world's oldest football was found in Stirling Castle.
Is this true? Aye or Naw?

Ewen Says: Aye
Twitter Says: Aye 74%; Naw 26%
You Say: **Aye** or **Naw?**

QUESTION 36
4.3.21

Ian Rankin, author of the famous Edinburgh-based
Inspector Rebus books, is from Fife. Is this true? Aye or Naw?

Ewen Says: Naw
Twitter Says: Aye 29%; Naw 71%
You Say: **Aye** or **Naw?**

QUESTION 37
5.3.21

Miss Jean Brodie was a real person.
Is this true? Aye or Naw?

Ewen Says: Aye
Twitter Says: Aye 66%; Naw 34%
You Say: **Aye** or **Naw?**

QUESTION 38
8.3.21 – International Women's Day

My Granny Jean flew over Rothesay in a plane
in the 1920s. Is this true? Aye or Naw?

Ewen Says: Naw
Twitter Says: Aye 32%; Naw 68%
You Say: **Aye** or **Naw?**

QUESTION 39
9.3.21

There are more sheep than people in Scotland.
Is this true? Aye or Naw?

Ewen Says: Aye
Twitter Says: Aye 51%; Naw 49%
You Say: **Aye** or **Naw?**

QUESTION 40
10.3.21

There are more pigs than cows in Scotland.
Is this true? Aye or Naw?

Ewen Says: Naw
Twitter Says: Aye 38%; Naw 62%
You Say: **Aye** or **Naw?**

QUESTION 41
11.3.21

There are more goats than Highland cows in Scotland.
Is this true? Aye or Naw?

Ewen Says: Aye
Twitter Says: Aye 44%; Naw 56%
You Say: **Aye** or **Naw?**

QUESTION 42
12.3.21

There is iron in Irn-Bru. Is this true? Aye or Naw?

Ewen Says: Naw
Twitter Says: Aye 47%; Naw 53%
You Say: **Aye** or **Naw?**

QUESTION 43
15.3.21 – The ides of March

There was a Caesar's Palace in Aberdeen.
Is this true? Aye or Naw?

Ewen Says: Aye (*He thought it was a shop, a garage or a Chinese restaurant, go figure!*)
Twitter Says: Aye 72%; Naw 28%
You Say: **Aye** or **Naw?**

QUESTION 44
16.3.21

A Scottish cheese was banned in Italy for being too powerful an aphrodisiac. Is this true? Aye or Naw?

Ewen Says: Naw
Twitter Says: Aye 42%; Naw 58%
You Say: **Aye** or **Naw?**

QUESTION 45
17.3.21 – St Patrick's Day

St Patrick was born in Scotland. Is this true? Aye or Naw?

Ewen Says: Naw
Twitter Says: Aye 14%; Naw 86%
You Say: **Aye** or **Naw?**

QUESTION 46
18.3.21

Scotland includes over nine hundred islands.
Is this true? Aye or Naw?

Ewen Says: Naw
Twitter Says: Aye 75%; Naw 25%
You Say: **Aye** or **Naw?**

QUESTION 47
19.3.21

Robert the Bruce once chipped his tooth with a coin
found in a dumpling. Is this true? Aye or Naw?

Ewen Says: Aye
Twitter Says: Aye 47%; Naw 53%
You Say: **Aye** or **Naw?**

QUESTION 48
29.3.21

Brora was the first place in the north of Scotland to have electricity. Is this true? Aye or Naw?

Ewen Says: Aye
Twitter Says: Aye 61%; Naw 39%
You Say: **Aye** or **Naw?**

QUESTION 49
30.3.21

Before finding fame, Marti Pellow started training as a plumber, this is why the band became 'Wet Wet Wet'. Is this true? Aye or Naw?

Ewen Says: Aye
Twitter Says: Aye 62% 38%
You Say: **Aye** or **Naw?**

QUESTION 50
31.3.21

Scotland manager Stevie Clark, along with two players, had 'Yes Sir, I Can Boogie' tattoos after qualifying for the Euros. Is this true? Aye or Naw?

Ewen Says: Naw
Twitter Says: Aye 11%; Naw 89%
You Say: **Aye** or **Naw?**

Congratulations! You've made it through the first fifty questions unscathed and will now be able to tell all your pals dazzling facts about penguins, Irn-Bru, curry, welly boots and horny cheese.

Turn to page 225 for the answers

Can You Go to the Pub and End Up Hosting a Stadium Gig?

Aye or Naw?

Picture the scene. I was in Johnny Foxes bar in Inverness dancing with my radio besties Arlene from Forth One and wee Vixen, AKA big boss Victoria. It's 12.41 a.m., I'm on a carefree girlie weekend break, a few Proseccos in, giving it laldi on the dance floor, and the text comes in: 'You're going to have to open for Duran Duran tomorrow.'

I looked at it again. It was from Ewen. Was he winding me up? He was booked to perform the all-important atmosphere building DJ set in the Caledonian Stadium in front of 10,000 people. He'd been back at work post-Covid and we thought he was fine, but he was shattered and put out his distress call to three half-cut party animals on their holidays.

Now, sensible people might have called it a day in anticipation of their highly unexpected high-profile forthcoming gig. Vixen, Arlene and I have never been sensible people. We got back to the hotel at 3.30 a.m., and I woke up the following morning wondering if I had dreamed the entire scenario.

We decided over sausages that Arlene and I would co-host the event. Neither of us had a laptop, so we made an eighties playlist on a phone for the sound desk. Nor did we have our usual sparkly stage clothes, so I presented wearing Primark jeggings, an M&S shirt and old boots. We looked and sounded like we'd been out until 3 a.m.

However, we decided to come clean right at the start and admitted to the audience that we only found out about our hosting duties in the pub after midnight and decided to stay out anyway – that got the biggest cheer of the day. I love Scotland!

What a laugh it turned out to be working the stage, saying hello to far-travelled fans, giving shoutouts to all the superfans and laughing at the hideous hastily assembled 'CAT AND ARLENE' graphic somebody somewhere had cut and pasted together and projected onto giant screens next to the main stage.

We looked like a poster for Menopause – The Movie! Despite our fragile status, I think we pulled it off, we got warm-up act Jack Savoretti on stage at exactly the right time and Duran Duran were magnificent.

We didn't get to meet them unfortunately as the stage manager had been so grateful that we stood in for Ewen at such short notice, he gave us sixteen free cocktail vouchers . . . and you'll guess how that turned out! 'Ordinary world'? I don't think so . . .

So, did I go to the pub and end up opening for Duran Duran? AYE!

April – June 2021

QUESTION 51
1.4.21

Ewen Cameron once worked as an exotic male dancer in a nightclub in Dubai. Is this true? Aye or Naw?

Ewen Says: Naw (*But is he lying?*)
Twitter Says: Aye 71%; Naw 29%
You Say: **Aye** or **Naw**?

QUESTION 52
2.4.21

The Scotch egg was invented in England. Is this true? Aye or Naw?

Ewen Says: Naw
Twitter Says: Aye 54%; Naw 46 %
You Say: **Aye** or **Naw**?

QUESTION 53
6.4.21

As of today, there have been more episodes of *River City* than *Take the High Road*. Is this true? Aye or Naw?

Ewen Says: Naw
Twitter Says: Aye 66 %; Naw 34%
You Say: **Aye** or **Naw**?

QUESTION 54
7.4.21

TV show *Supergran* became a massive hit in Cuba and China. Is this true? Aye or Naw?

Ewen Says: Naw
Twitter Says: Aye 50%; Naw 50%
You Say: **Aye** or **Naw**?

QUESTION 55
8.4.21

Despite finishing in 2008, STV's *Scotsport* remains the longest running sports show in history.
Is this true? Aye or Naw?

Ewen Says: Naw
Twitter Says: Aye 31%; Naw 61%
You Say: **Aye** or **Naw**?

QUESTION 56
9.4.21

Before becoming a detective, Jim Taggart (from *Taggart*) was once a criminal who stole Jimmy Shand records from his local Woolworths. Is this true? Aye or Naw?

Ewen Says: Naw
Twitter Says: Aye 11%; Naw 89%
You Say: **Aye** or **Naw**?

QUESTION 57
12.4.21

The majority of the horses used in the fight scenes in the Oscar-winning movie *Braveheart* were fake. Is this true? Aye or Naw?

Ewen Says: Aye
Twitter Says: Aye 58%; Aye 19%
You Say: **Aye** or **Naw**?

QUESTION 58
14.4.21

In the film *Ring of Bright Water*, some of the scenes featuring Mij the otter were filmed using a giant black pudding with sticky-on eyes. Is this true? Aye or Naw?

Ewen Says: Aye
Twitter Says: Aye 78%; Naw 22%
You Say: **Aye** or **Naw**?

QUESTION 59
19.4.21

Blair Drummond Safari Park was opened in 1970 by James Bond star Sean Connory, who was pictured cutting the ribbon with a lion cub and a baby giraffe. Is this true? Aye or Naw?

Ewen Says: Aye
Twitter Says: Aye 77%; Naw 23%
You Say: **Aye** or **Naw**?

QUESTION 60
20.4.21

Edinburgh Castle was once home to an elephant that loved beer. Is this true? Aye or Naw?

Ewen Says: Naw
Twitter Says: Aye 53%; Naw 47%
You Say: **Aye** or **Naw**?

QUESTION 61
21.4.21

Annie Lennox once got lost in Scotland's oldest maze in Hazlehead Park in Aberdeen and needed the park keeper to guide her out. Is this true? Aye or Naw?

Ewen Says: Aye
Twitter Says: Aye 76%; Naw 24%
You Say: **Aye** or **Naw**?

QUESTION 62
22.4.21

Moat Brae, the Peter Pan house in Dumfries, has a real baby crocodile called Tick Tock in the petting zoo behind the house. Is this true? Aye or Naw?

Ewen Says: Aye
Twitter Says: Aye 37%; Naw 63%
You Say: **Aye** or **Naw**?

QUESTION 63
23.4.21

John o' Groats is NOT the most Northerly point of mainland Scotland. Is this true? Aye or Naw?

Ewen Says: Naw
Twitter Says: Aye 58%; Naw 42%
You Say: **Aye** or **Naw**?

QUESTION 64

26.4.21 – Gyms are allowed to open again today following Covid restrictions.

The rowing machine is the most popular machine in a gym. Is this true? Aye or Naw?

Ewen Says: Naw
Twitter Says: Aye 10%; Naw 90%
You Say: **Aye** or **Naw**?

QUESTION 65
27.4.21

Scotland has more castles than any other country.
Is this true? Aye or Naw?

Ewen Says: Naw
Twitter Says: Aye 64%; Naw 36%
You Say: **Aye** or **Naw**?

QUESTION 66
28.4.21

In Scotland it is illegal to be drunk in charge of a donkey.
Is this true? Aye or Naw?

Ewen Says: Aye
Twitter Says: Aye 79%; Naw 21%
You Say: **Aye** or **Naw**?

QUESTION 67
29.4.21

Only lady midges have teeth. Is this true? Aye or Naw?

Ewen Says: Naw
Twitter Says: Aye 47%; Naw 53%
You Say: **Aye** or **Naw**?

QUESTION 68
30.4.21

My dad once woke up on the floor of a Partick Thistle manager's house cuddling the Scottish Cup.
Is this true? Aye or Naw?

Ewen Says: Aye
Twitter Says: Aye 78%; Naw 22%
You Say: **Aye** or **Naw**?

QUESTION 69
10.5.21

There is no such thing as pear cider.
Is this true? Aye or Naw?

Ewen Says: Naw
Twitter Says: Aye 36%; Naw 64%
You Say: **Aye** or **Naw**?

QUESTION 70
11.5.21

Humans are the only animal species that blush.
Is this true? Aye or Naw?

Ewen Says: Aye
Twitter Says: Aye 35%; Naw 65%
You Say: **Aye** or **Naw**?

QUESTION 71
12.5.21

Candy floss was invented by a dentist.
Is this true? Aye or Naw?

Ewen Says: Naw
Twitter Says: Aye 47%; Naw 53%
You Say: **Aye** or **Naw**?

QUESTION 72
13.5.21

According to scientists, the Isle of Skye is the best place in the world to see rainbows. Is this true? Aye or Naw?

Ewen Says: Aye
Twitter Says: Aye 62%; Naw 38%
You Say: **Aye** or **Naw**?

QUESTION 73
14.5.21

The inventor of the famous Pringles tube got buried in a Pringles tube when he died. Is this true? Aye or Naw?

Ewen Says: Naw
Twitter Says: Aye 32%; Naw 68%
You Say: **Aye** or **Naw**?

QUESTION 74
17.5.21

Bumblebees can fly higher than Mount Everest. Is this true? Aye or Naw?

Ewen Says: Naw
Twitter Says: Aye 28%; Naw 72%
You Say: **Aye** or **Naw**?

QUESTION 75
18.5.21

The most popular colour of toilet paper in
France is pink. Is this true? Aye or Naw?

Ewen Says: Naw
Twitter Says: Aye 46%; Naw 54%
You Say: **Aye** or **Naw**?

QUESTION 76
19.5.21

The Canary Islands are named after dogs, not birds.
Is this true? Aye or Naw?

Ewen Says: Naw
Twitter Says: Aye 53%; Naw 47%
You Say: **Aye** or **Naw**?

QUESTION 77
20.5.21

Rottweilers were once used to pull canal boats
in Germany. Is this true? Aye or Naw?

Ewen Says: Aye
Twitter Says: Aye 48%; Naw 52%
You Say: **Aye** or **Naw**?

QUESTION 78
21.5.21

Yoda in *Star Wars* was originally meant to be played by a monkey wearing a mask. Is this true? Aye or Naw?

Ewen Says: Aye
Twitter Says: Aye 33%; Naw 67%
You Say: **Aye** or **Naw**?

QUESTION 79
24.5.21 – National Asparagus Day

Everyone can make 'asparagus pee' but not everyone can smell it. Is this true? Aye or Naw?

Ewen Says: Naw
Twitter Says: Aye 69%; Naw 31%
You Say: **Aye** or **Naw**?

QUESTION 80
25.5.21 – National Tap Dance Day

Tap dancing was invented by a plumber working on a New York construction site in the 1800s. He tied shards of metal to his shoes to entertain colleagues during their breaks. Is this true? Aye or Naw?

Ewen Says: Aye
Twitter Says: Aye 38%; Naw 62%
You Say: **Aye** or **Naw**?

QUESTION 81
26.5.21 – Stevie Nicks' 73rd birthday

Fleetwood Mac's Stevie Nicks helped run her family
bicycle shop before taking up music full-time.
Is this true? Aye or Naw?

Ewen Says: Aye
Twitter Says: Aye 70%; Naw 30%
You Say: **Aye** or **Naw**?

QUESTION 82
27.5.21

The state of Texas is bigger than every individual
European country. Is this true? Aye or Naw?

Ewen Says: Naw
Twitter Says: Aye 69%; Naw 31%
You Say: **Aye** or **Naw**?

QUESTION 83
28.5.21

A langoustine is a prawn, not a lobster.
Is this true? Aye or Naw?

Ewen Says: Aye
Twitter Says: Aye 76%; Naw 24%
You Say: **Aye** or **Naw**?

QUESTION 84
8.6.21

Caterpillars have eight eyes. Is this true? Aye or Naw?

Ewen Says: Aye
Twitter Says: Aye 31%; Naw 69%
You Say: **Aye** or **Naw**?

QUESTION 85
9.6.21 – Donald Duck Day

Donald Duck has a middle name.
Is this true? Aye or Naw?

Ewen Says: Aye
Twitter Says: Aye 55%; Naw 45%
You Say: **Aye** or **Naw**?

QUESTION 86
10.6.21

In Japan, golfers buy insurance to financially
protect themselves if they get a hole in one.
Is this true? Aye or Naw?

Ewen Says: Naw
Twitter Says: Aye 68%; Naw 32%
You Say: **Aye** or **Naw**?

QUESTION 87
11.6.21 – The EUROS commence.

More people live in Italy than Turkey.
Is this true? Aye or Naw?

Ewen Says: Aye
Twitter Says: Aye 35%; Naw 65%
You Say: **Aye** or **Naw**?

QUESTION 88
14.6.21

Chess was invented in the old Czechoslovakia.
That is why when you win, you say: 'Czech mate.'
Is this true? Aye or Naw?

Ewen Says: Aye
Twitter Says: Aye 19%; Naw 81%
You Say: **Aye** or **Naw**?

QUESTION 89
15.6.21

French is spoken by more people than Portuguese.
Is this true? Aye or Naw?

Ewen Says: Aye
Twitter Says: Aye 43%; Naw 57%
You Say: **Aye** or **Naw**?

QUESTION 90
16.6.21 – Turkey v Wales

Turkeys have more bones than whales.
Is this true? Aye or Naw?

Ewen Says: Aye
Twitter Says: Aye 40%; Naw 60%
You Say: **Aye** or **Naw**?

QUESTION 91
17.6.21 – Denmark v Belgium

Belgians eat more chocolate than any other
country in Europe. Is this true? Aye or Naw?

Ewen Says: Aye
Twitter Says: Aye 59%; Naw 41%
You Say: **Aye** or **Naw**?

QUESTION 92
21.6.21

Finland is officially the happiest country in the world.
Is this true? Aye or Naw?

Ewen Says: Naw
Twitter Says: Aye 42%; Naw 58%
You Say: **Aye** or **Naw**?

QUESTION 93
22.6.21 – Skerryvore play in our studio ahead of
Croatia v Scotland

Skerryvore is Gaelic for 'handsome men'.
Is this true? Aye or Naw?

Ewen Says: Naw
Twitter Says: Aye 25%; Naw 75%
You Say: **Aye** or **Naw**?

QUESTION 94
23.6.21

Poland is the natural habitat of Europe's heaviest
type of animal. Is this true? Aye or Naw?

Ewen Says: Naw
Twitter Says: Aye 44%; Naw 56%
You Say: **Aye** or **Naw**?

QUESTION 95
24.6.21

Danish Pastries are not from Denmark.
Is this true? Aye or Naw?

Ewen Says: Naw
Twitter Says: Aye 52%; Naw 48%
You Say: **Aye** or **Naw**?

QUESTION 96
25.6.21

There is a free wine fountain in Italy offering as much red wine as you'd like, twenty-four hours a day, seven days a week. Is this true? Aye or Naw?

Ewen Says: Naw
Twitter Says: Aye 30%; Naw 70%
You Say: **Aye** or **Naw**?

QUESTION 97
28.6.21

Spain produces more olive oil than any other country. Is this true? Aye or Naw?

Ewen Says: Aye
Twitter Says: Aye 51%; Naw 49%
You Say: **Aye** or **Naw**?

QUESTION 98
29.6.21

Germans drink more beer per person than any other European country. Is this true? Aye or Naw?

Ewen Says: Aye
Twitter Says: Aye 52%; Naw 48%
You Say: **Aye** or **Naw**?

Chicken Kiev was invented in the Ukrainian capital.
Is this true? Aye or Naw?

Ewen Says: Aye
Twitter Says: Aye 24%; Naw 76%
You Say: **Aye** or **Naw**?

Woo hoo – you are nearly one hundred useless facts better off. Add elephants, Donald Duck, Pringles, rainbows and pink loo rolls to your new list of specialist subjects!

Answers on page 229

River City and Ewen —
Could He Win a BAFTA?

Aye or Naw?

Scottish soap *River City* has been on our screens for over twenty years and the much-loved show invited us to witness life on Montego Street for ourselves.

We agreed to film and record behind the scenes with some of the biggest stars; Stephen Purdon (Shellsuit Bob), Joyce Falconer (Roisin), Scott Fletcher (Angus), Jordon Young (Alex Murdoch), Gayle Telfer Stevens (Caitlin), Sally Howitt (Scarlett), Frank Gallagher (Lenny Murdoch) and Jacqueline Leonard (Lydia Murdoch).

We have known and interviewed most of them many times over the years and count them as good friends. In particular, Stephen and I go way back, we've performed in over six hundred of the same pantos together at the Pavilion and shared many a crazy night out.

After we had all the material we needed, Julie the lovely *River City* Press Officer asked if we wanted to BE in the show.

Ewen was starstruck: 'Who shall I be, is it a big part?'

Julie explained: 'You can be extras at the coffee stand and just have to pick up your drinks and walk over the road.'

You'd think we'd be able to smash that no bother at all.

The assistant director told us just to look natural as we walked over the street chatting to each other, but not saying anything out loud. That was too tricky a concept for Ewen.

On take one he looked terrified with eyes popping, while on take two he walked in front of a moving car and the director had to shout, 'CUT – WATCH WHERE YOU ARE GOING.' Take three was fine: by then I told him NOT to pretend to talk, just listen to me pretend to talk.

Honestly, three-take extras! I am not expecting a call back anytime soon.

When the show was eventually aired, we are two little dots in the far distance. I'm usually quite modest but I'm proud to admit I crossed that road clutching a fake coffee like a pro!

So, will Ewen get a BAFTA for his *River City* debut?
NAW!

July – Sep 2021

QUESTION 100
1.7.21

Switzerland owns a greater percentage of the Alps than any other country. Is this true? Aye or Naw?

Ewen Says: Aye
Twitter Says: Aye 58%; Naw 42%
You Say: **Aye** or **Naw**?

QUESTION 101
2.7.21

The Italian dessert tiramisu means 'pick me up' as it contains so many high-energy ingredients like sugar, eggs and espresso. Is this true? Aye or Naw?

Ewen Says: Aye
Twitter Says: Aye 57%; Naw 43%
You Say: **Aye** or **Naw**?

QUESTION 102
5.7.21

The sound of a Spanish donkey's bray can carry up to 100 miles in the desert. Is this true? Aye or Naw?

Ewen Says: Naw

Twitter Says: Aye 47%; Naw 53%

You Say: **Aye** or **Naw**

QUESTION 103
6.7.21

Americans eat more pasta per person than Italians. Is this true? Aye or Naw?

Ewen Says: Aye

Twitter Says: Aye 64%; Naw 36%

You Say: **Aye** or **Naw**?

QUESTION 104
7.7.21

Whigfield's famous hit 'Saturday Night' was originally recorded as 'Friday Night'. Is this true? Aye or Naw?

Ewen Says: Aye

Twitter Says: Aye 24%; Naw 76%

You Say: **Aye** or **Nee Nee Na Na Naw**? (I made myself laugh with that one!)

QUESTION 105
8.7.21

England manager Gareth Southgate could have represented his country competing at high jump but chose to focus on football instead. Is this true? Aye or Naw?

Ewen Says: Aye
Twitter Says: Aye 59%; Naw 41%
You Say: **Aye** or **Naw**?

QUESTION 106
9.7.21

Pavarotti has sold more records than Status Quo. Is this true? Aye or Naw?

Ewen Says: Aye
Twitter Says: Aye 75%; Naw 25%
You Say: **Aye** or **Naw**?

QUESTION 107
26.7.21 – The Covid-19 delayed Tokyo 2020 Olympics started on 23 July 2021

Athletes in the ancient Olympic Games uses to compete in the nude. Is this true? Aye or Naw?

Ewen Says: Aye
Twitter Says: Aye 62%; Naw 38%
You Say: **Aye** or **Naw**?

QUESTION 108
27.7.21

This year's Olympic Gold medals are made from recycled mobile phones. Is this true? Aye or Naw?

Ewen Says: Naw
Twitter Says: Aye 49%; Naw 51%
You Say: **Aye** or **Naw**?

QUESTION 109
28.7.21

The 60m pogo-stick race formed part of the 1904 summer Olympics in St Louis, Missouri. Is this true? Aye or Naw?

Ewen Says: Aye
Twitter Says: Aye 30%; Naw 70%
You Say: **Aye** or **Naw**?

QUESTION 110
29.7.21

Pankration was one of the original sports in the ancient Olympics. It involved running a mile carrying a large rock. Is this true? Aye or Naw?

Ewen Says: Naw
Twitter Says: Aye 55%; Naw 45%
You Say: **Aye** or **Naw**?

QUESTION 111
30.7.21

Underwater swimming in the Seine was a sport in the 1900 Paris Olympics. Is this true? Aye or Naw?

Ewen Says: Naw
Twitter Says: Aye 56%; Naw 46%
You Say: **Aye** or **Naw**?

QUESTION 112
2.8.21

Fortune cookies originated in China. Is this true? Aye or Naw?

Ewen Says: Aye
Twitter Says: Aye 59%; Naw 41%
You Say: **Aye** or **Naw**?

QUESTION 113
3.8.21

The sport of pole vaulting started as a way to cross canals in the Netherlands. Is this true? Aye or Naw?

Ewen Says: Naw
Twitter Says: Aye 65%; Naw 35%
You Say: **Aye** or **Naw**?

QUESTION 114
4.8.21

The athletes at the Olympics are sleeping on cardboard.
Is this true? Aye or Naw?

Ewen Says: Aye
Twitter Says: Aye 65%; Naw 35%
You Say: **Aye** or **Naw**?

QUESTION 115
5.8.21

Only three athletes have achieved gold medals in both the
summer and winter Olympics. Is this true? Aye or Naw?

Ewen Says: Aye
Twitter Says: Aye 74%; Naw 26%
You Say: **Aye** or **Naw**?

QUESTION 116
6.8.21

Sir Chris Hoy, who has seven Olympic medals,
was inspired to cycle after watching *E.T.*
Is this true? Aye or Naw?

Ewen Says: Naw
Twitter Says: Aye 55%; Naw 45%
You Say: **Aye** or **Naw**?

QUESTION 117
9.8.21

Worms have excellent hearing. Is this true? Aye or Naw?

Ewen Says: Aye
Twitter Says: Aye 42%; Naw 58%
You Say: **Aye** or **Naw**?

QUESTION 118
10.8.21

There is a breed of dog that can't bark but can yodel.
Is this true? Aye or Naw?

Ewen Says: Naw
Twitter Says: Aye 40%; Naw 60%
You Say: **Aye** or **Naw**?

QUESTION 119
11.8.21

Acrophobia, the fear of heights, is the most common
phobia in the world. Is this true? Aye or Naw?

Ewen Says: Aye
Twitter Says: Aye 40%; Naw 60%
You Say: **Aye** or **Naw**?

QUESTION 120
12.8.21

The most expensive cheese in the world is made of donkey milk. Is this true? Aye or Naw?

Ewen Says: Naw
Twitter Says: Aye 34%; Naw 66%
You Say: **Aye** or **Naw**?

QUESTION 121
13.8.21

There is a type of cat from the Brazilian rainforest that can fly. Is this true? Aye or Naw?

Ewen Says: Aye
Twitter Says: Aye 37%; Naw 63%
You Say: **Aye** or **Naw**?

QUESTION 122
16.8.21 – National Roller Coaster Day

'The Big One' in Blackpool is Europe's highest roller coaster. Is this true? Aye or Naw?

Ewen Says: Aye
Twitter Says: Aye 33%; Naw 67%
You Say: **Aye** or **Naw**?

QUESTION 123
17.8.21

Cartoon favourites Tom and Jerry are named
after a cocktail. Is this true? Aye or Naw?

Ewen Says: Naw
Twitter Says: Aye 30%; Naw 70%
You Say: **Aye** or **Naw**?

QUESTION 124
18.8.21

Goldfish can recognise their owners.
Is this true? Aye or Naw?

Ewen Says: Aye
Twitter Says: Aye 33%; Naw 67%
You Say: **Aye** or **Naw**?

QUESTION 125
19.8.21

The real James Bond was an American author who wrote
books about exotic birds. Is this true? Aye or Naw?

Ewen Says: Naw
Twitter Says: Aye 34%; Naw 66%
You Say: **Aye** or **Naw**?

QUESTION 126
20.8.21

Termites fart more than cows. Is this true? Aye or Naw?

Ewen Says: Naw
Twitter Says: Aye 57%; Naw 43%
You Say: **Aye** or **Naw**?

It is impossible to hum while holding your nose.
Is this true? Aye or Naw?

Ewen Says: Aye
Twitter Says: Aye 55%; Naw 45%
You Say: **Aye** or **Naw**?

September comes from the Latin word for 'seven',
as it was the seventh month in the calendar.
Is this true? Aye or Naw?

Ewen Says: Naw
Twitter Says: Aye 66%; Naw 34%
You Say: **Aye** or **Naw**?

The average person uses the toilet more than
four thousand times a year. Is this true? Aye or Naw?

Ewen Says: Aye
Twitter Says: Aye 65%; Naw 35%
You Say: **Aye** or **Naw**?

QUESTION 130
16.9.21

Before he was famous, Pulp frontman Jarvis Cocker used to scrub crabs. Is this true? Aye or Naw?

Ewen Says: Naw
Twitter Says: Aye 67%; Naw 33%
You Say: **Aye** or **Naw**?

QUESTION 131
17.9.21

More people can roll their tongues than can't. Is this true? Aye or Naw?

Ewen Says: Aye
Twitter Says: Aye 48%; Naw 52%
You Say: **Aye** or **Naw**?

QUESTION 132
20.9.21

Before he was famous, David Bowie was a gravedigger in London. Is this true? Aye or Naw?

Ewen Says: Aye
Twitter Says: Aye 67%; Naw 33%
You Say: **Aye** or **Naw**?

QUESTION 133
21.9.21 – The Great British Bake Off returns to our screens

The first ever wedding cake was made of bread.
Is this true? Aye or Naw?

Ewen Says: Aye
Twitter Says: Aye 77%; Naw 23%
You Say: **Aye** or **Naw**?

QUESTION 134
22.9.21 – Elephant Appreciation Day

Elephants' tusks are actually big teeth.
Is this true? Aye or Naw?

Ewen Says: Aye
Twitter Says: Aye 37%; Naw 63%
You Say: **Aye** or **Naw**?

QUESTION 135
23.9.21

Today's date, 23 September, is the busiest day
for births in the UK. Is this true? Aye or Naw?

Ewen Says: Aye
Twitter Says: Aye 70%; Naw 30%
You Say: **Aye** or **Naw**?

QUESTION 136
24.9.21

The funny bone is not a bone. Is this true? Aye or Naw?

Ewen Says: Naw
Twitter Says: Aye 59%; Naw 41%
You Say: **Aye** or **Naw**?

QUESTION 137
27.9.21 – TV submarine drama *Vigil* launches

China has more submarines than any other country.
Is this true? Aye or Naw?

Ewen Says: Aye
Twitter Says: Aye 54%; Naw 46%
You Say: **Aye** or **Naw**?

QUESTION 138
28.9.21

The Portuguese drink more hot chocolate than any
other country. Is this true? Aye or Naw?

Ewen Says: Naw
Twitter Says: Aye 42%; Naw 58%
You Say: **Aye** or **Naw**?

QUESTION 139
29.9.21

The M6 is made of books. Is this true? Aye or Naw?

Ewen Says: Naw
Twitter Says: Aye 26%; Naw 74%
You Say: **Aye** or **Naw**?

QUESTION 140
30.9.21 – Michael Bolton plays Glasgow

Michael Bolton's first professional gig was as an opera singer. Is this true? Aye or Naw?

Ewen Says: Aye
Twitter Says: Aye 59%; Naw 41%
You Say: **Aye** or **Naw**?

So as this summer comes to an end, I've now taught you about donkeys, pasta, worms, Latin words, yodelling dogs and farting beasties. You are welcome!

Answers on page 233

Can Potatoes Make Good Pets?

Aye or Naw?

This has to be one of my favourite subjects of the year. Ewen was appalled to learn that I once had a pet potato when I was about five.

I wanted a hamster, parents said no, so I drew a hamster's face on a potato, named him 'Potamster' and tried to prove I was capable of looking after a pet.

Imagination is a beautiful thing and thankfully you lot came to my rescue with similar stories of curiously inventive creatures.

A special shoutout to Ray Kinnaird, Alison Fitzsimmons, Suzy Kerr and Stephanie Forsyth, who also, rather astonishingly, had pet potatoes!

Tracy had a bath plug on a chain she dragged everywhere as her dog.

Karen kept pet worms Wiggles, Wig and Wobbly in a fish tank. They were made of spaghetti and her mum didn't have the heart to fling them out.

Gillian Campbell's daughter had a pet brick called James.

Lynn kept a Vosene shampoo bottle in a sock and named him Vosy Posy, while Perry called in to say her nephew

Kenny Miller gave his daughter a cage with bedding and a coconut lying on top.

Emily looked after the coconut for years before it was replaced with a real-life hamster.

Tracey from Dumfries had both of us crying with laughter when she told us about her sister's unusual pet: 'Linda had a pet polar bear. I mean he clearly wasn't a polar bear, but she told everyone that he was. He was a big cement drum on a rope called Grizzles that she dragged everywhere with her. She loved him very much.'

I bet – like polar bears – Grizzles broke the ice wherever he turned up . . .

So, can potatoes make good pets?
Well, Potamster lasted about five weeks, turned squishy, green and wrinkly, and started to grow shoots out his head. He was cheap to feed and didn't require much (any) exercise, but I am going to have to say –
NAW!

Oct – Dec 2021

QUESTION 141

4.10.21 – My second book, *Cat's Out the Bag*, is launched this week. It became an Amazon No. 1 bestseller with all proceeds going to Cash for Kids. Thank you. So, this week was book themed.

Danish people read more than folk from any other country. Is this true? Aye or Naw?

Ewen Says: Aye
Twitter Says: Aye 73%; Naw 27%
You Say: **Aye** or **Naw**?

QUESTION 142
5.10.21

Oor Wullie annuals came out before *Beano* annuals. Is this true? Aye or Naw?

Ewen Says: Aye
Twitter Says: Aye 48%; Naw 52%
You Say: **Aye** or **Naw**?

QUESTION 143
6.10.21

Mr Happy was the very first book in the
Mr Men series. Is this true? Aye or Naw?

Ewen Says: Aye
Twitter Says: Aye 65%; Naw 35%
You Say: **Aye** or **Naw**?

QUESTION 144
7.10.21

There are more Enid Blyton *Secret Seven* books
than *Famous Five* books. Is this true? Aye or Naw?

Ewen Says: Aye
Twitter Says: Aye 49%; Naw 51%
You Say: **Aye** or **Naw**?

QUESTION 145
8.10.21

In JK Rowling's first draft, Harry Potter was originally
named 'Barry Potter'. Is this true? Aye or Naw?

Ewen Says: Naw
Twitter Says: Aye 14%; Naw 86%
You Say: **Aye** or **Naw**?

QUESTION 146
18.10.21 – Alaska Day

There are more bears than people in Alaska.
Is this true? Aye or Naw?

Ewen Says: Aye
Twitter Says: Aye 53%; Naw 47%
You Say: **Aye** or **Naw**?

QUESTION 147
19.10.21

The Spice Girls had more UK No. 1's than Take That.
Is this true? Aye or Naw?

Ewen Says: Aye
Twitter Says: Aye 48%; Naw 52%
You Say: **Aye** or **Naw**?

QUESTION 148
20.10.21

Turtles can grow out of their shells when they grow
too big for them. Is this true? Aye or Naw?

Ewen Says: Naw
Twitter Says: Aye 11%; Naw 89%
You Say: **Aye** or **Naw**?

QUESTION 149
21.10.21 – Kim Kardashian's birthday

Before finding fame, Kim Kardashian trained dolphins.
Is this true? Aye or Naw?

Ewen Says: Aye
Twitter Says: Aye 71%; Naw 29%
You Say: **Aye** or **Naw**?

QUESTION 150
25.10.21

According to Google, the most popular Halloween
outfit of 2021 will be a witch. Is this true? Aye or Naw?

Ewen Says: Naw
Twitter Says: Aye 48%; Naw 52%
You Say: **Aye** or **Naw**?

QUESTION 151
26.10.21

The Count from *Sesame Street* is over a
million years old. Is this true? Aye or Naw?

Ewen Says: Naw
Twitter Says: Aye 48%; Naw 52%
You Say: **Aye** or **Naw**?

QUESTION 152
27.10.21

Chucky, the scary doll from the *Child's Play* film series
was based on the cute cabbage patch dolls from the 1980s.
Is this true? Aye or Naw?

Ewen Says: Aye
Twitter Says: Aye 60%; Naw 40%
You Say: **Aye** or **Naw**?

QUESTION 153
29.10.21

The heaviest pumpkin grown this year weighs more than
two Aberdeen Angus cows. Is this true? Aye or Naw?

Ewen Says: Naw
Twitter Says: Aye 33%; Naw 67%
You Say: **Aye** or **Naw**?

QUESTION 154
1.11.21 – COP26, the climate conference, begins

COP26 is now underway in Glasgow. COP stands for
Conserve Our Planet. Is this true? Aye or Naw?

Ewen Says: Aye
Twitter Says: Aye 33%; Naw 67%
You Say: **Aye** or **Naw**?

QUESTION 155
2.11.21 – Joe Biden is speaking at COP26

US President Joe Biden once spent $10,000
on ice cream. Is this true? Aye or Naw?

Ewen Says: Aye
Twitter Says: Aye 54%; Naw 46%
You Say: **Aye** or **Naw**?

QUESTION 156
3.11.21 – Security is high at COP26

SWAT stands for Secret Weapons Advanced Team.
Is this true? Aye or Naw?

Ewen Says: Naw
Twitter Says: Aye 19 %; Naw 81%
You Say: **Aye** or **Naw**?

QUESTION 157
4.11.21

The Pacific Ocean is the deepest in the world.
Is this true? Aye or Naw?

Ewen Says: Aye
Twitter Says: Aye 61%; Naw 39%
You Say: **Aye** or **Naw**?

QUESTION 158
5.11.21

Climate campaigner Greta Thunberg's mum once represented Sweden at the Eurovision Song Contest. Is this true? Aye or Naw?

Ewen Says: Naw
Twitter Says: Aye 47%; Naw 53%
You Say: **Aye** or **Naw**?

QUESTION 159
8.11.21 – Obama arrives at COP26

Barack Obama has three Grammys. Is this true? Aye or Naw?

Ewen Says: Naw
Twitter Says: Aye 24%; Naw 76%
You Say: **Aye** or **Naw**?

QUESTION 160
9.11.21 – Women's Day at COP26

There are twice as many women as men in Alaska. Is this true? Aye or Naw?

Ewen Says: Aye
Twitter Says: Aye 54%; Naw 46%
You Say: **Aye** or **Naw**?

QUESTION 161
10.11.21

There are more registered cars on the road in the
UK than in Germany. Is this true? Aye or Naw?

Ewen Says: Aye
Twitter Says: Aye 57%; Naw 43%
You Say: **Aye** or **Naw**?

QUESTION 162
11.11.21

It costs more to make a coffee at home from a
machine than a tea at home from the kettle.
Is this true? Aye or Naw?

Ewen Says: Aye
Twitter Says: Aye 72%; Naw 28%
You Say: **Aye** or **Naw**?

QUESTION 163
12.11.21 – Moldova 0–2 Scotland, World Cup Qualifiers

The National dish of Moldova is porridge.
Is this true? Aye or Naw?

Ewen Says: Aye
Twitter Says: Aye 72%; Naw 28%
You Say: **Aye** or **Naw**?

QUESTION 164
15.11.21 – Scotland 2–0 Denmark, WCQ

Denmark and Scotland have the two oldest continuously used flags in the world. Is this true? Aye or Naw?

Ewen Says: Aye
Twitter Says: Aye 70%; Naw 30%
You Say: **Aye** or **Naw**?

QUESTION 165
16.11.21

Scotland star John Souttar's wee brother plays for Australia. Is this true? Aye or Naw?

Ewen Says: Aye
Twitter Says: Aye 71%; Naw 29%
You Say: **Aye** or **Naw**?

QUESTION 166
17.11.21 – Unfriend on Social Media Day

The average person has fewer than three hundred friends on Facebook. Is this true? Aye or Naw?

Ewen Says: Aye
Twitter Says: Aye 69%; Naw 31%
You Say: **Aye** or **Naw**?

QUESTION 167
18.11.21 – National Mickey Mouse Day

Mickey Mouse was originally meant to be called Montgommery Mouse. Is this true? Aye or Naw?

Ewen Says: Naw
Twitter Says: Aye 72%; Naw 28%
You Say: **Aye** or **Naw**?

QUESTION 168
19.11.21 – Monopoly Day

The longest game of Monopoly lasted over seventy days. Is this true? Aye or Naw?

Ewen Says: Naw
Twitter Says: Aye 72%; Naw 28%
You Say: **Aye** or **Naw**?

QUESTION 169
29.11.21 – Noel's House Party 30th Anniversary

Mr Blobby was originally inspired by a mouldy pork sausage. Is this true? Aye or Naw?

Ewen Says: Naw
Twitter Says: Aye 34%; Naw 66%
You Say: **Aye** or **Naw**?

QUESTION 170
6.12.21

The world record for the most sprouts individually consumed in one minute is over forty.
Is this true? Aye or Naw?

Ewen Says: Aye
Twitter Says: Aye 72%; Naw 28%
You Say: **Aye** or **Naw**?

QUESTION 171
7.12.21

Over 200 million crackers will be pulled in the UK this festive season. Is this true? Aye or Naw?

Ewen Says: Aye
Twitter Says: Aye 65%; Naw 35%
You Say: **Aye** or **Naw**?

QUESTION 172
8.12.21.

Reindeer are the only breed of deer to have hairy noses. Is this true? Aye or Naw?

Ewen Says: Aye
Twitter Says: Aye 43%; Naw 57%
You Say: **Aye** or **Naw**?

QUESTION 173
9.12.21

'White Christmas' is the bestselling Christmas song of all time. Is this true? Aye or Naw?

Ewen Says: Naw
Twitter Says: Aye 47%; Naw 53%
You Say: **Aye** or **Naw**?

QUESTION 174
10.11.21

'Jingle Bells' was the first song ever played in space. Is this true? Aye or Naw?

Ewen Says: Aye
Twitter Says: Aye 47%; Naw 53%
You Say: **Aye** or **Naw**?

QUESTION 175
13.12.21

A donkey can run faster than a reindeer. Is this true? Aye or Naw?

Ewen Says: Naw
Twitter Says: Aye 26%; Naw 74%
You Say: **Aye** or **Naw**?

QUESTION 176
14.12.21

The average snowman is 5ft or less.
Is this true? Aye or Naw?

Ewen Says: Aye
Twitter Says: Aye 80%; Naw 20%
You Say: **Aye** or **Naw**?

QUESTION 177
15.12.21

Monopoly is the bestselling Christmas toy
of all time. Is this true? Aye or Naw?

Ewen Says: Aye
Twitter Says: Aye 56%; Naw 44%
You Say: **Aye** or **Naw**?

QUESTION 178
16.12.21

The famous Rockefeller Christmas tree in New York
this year is taller than the rugby goal posts at Murrayfield.
Is this true? Aye or Naw?

Ewen Says: Aye
Twitter Says: Aye 80%; Naw 20%
You Say: **Aye** or **Naw**?

QUESTION 179
17.12.21

Home Alone is the highest grossing Christmas movie of all time Is this true? Aye or Naw?

Ewen Says: Aye
Twitter Says: Aye 62%; Naw 38%
You Say: **Aye** or **Naw**?

QUESTION 180
20.12.21

The average 6ft Christmas tree has over eighty baubles. Is this true? Aye or Naw?

Ewen Says: Aye
Twitter Says: Aye 47%; Naw 53%
You Say: **Aye** or **Naw**?

QUESTION 181
21.12.21

The tradition of kissing under mistletoe was started by Vikings. Is this true? Aye or Naw?

Ewen Says: Naw
Twitter Says: Aye 39%; Naw 61%
You Say: **Aye** or **Naw**?

Fresh reindeer droppings were once considered
an aphrodisiac by indigenous Nordic people.
Is this true? Aye or Naw?

Ewen Says: Aye
Twitter Says: Aye 57%; Naw 43%
You Say: **Aye** or **Naw**?

Ho ho hope you are getting these correct. Are you a
Christmas cracker or a big turkey?

Turn to page 237 for the answers

Can You Buy Dodgy Tickets from a Scottish TV Icon?

Aye or Naw?

Prepare for the dropping of many names in this celebrity tale of scandal, intrigue and mistaken identity. Ewen and I are lucky enough to be friends with many of the stars we've interviewed over the years.

My first love, Marti Pellow, is a regular on our show and kindly invited us to his amazing gig at the Armadillo in Glasgow. We invited *Still Game's* Victor aka Greg Hemphill and his lovely wife Miss Hoolie from *Balamory*, or Julie Wilson Nimmo in the real world, to join us.

Going out with Greg and Julie is hilarious because people stare and smile as they try to work out how they're familiar. When not dressed in character as a grumpy pensioner from *Craiglang* and a bubbly schoolteacher from children's TV hit *Balamory*, it can be confusing.

However, this led to one of the highlights of my year.

Greg, Julie, Producer Cat and I were standing outside the venue waiting for Ewen to pick up our tickets from the box office. Greg had his coat buttoned up to the neck, a tweed cap pulled down over his eyes and a thick bushy beard. He looked shifty!

This woman came up to him and said: 'You're HIM, aren't you? You are, yes? You are, I know you are!' Greg, not wanting to assume she knew he was Victor from the telly who had written and performed a show that sold out the adjacent Hydro a record fifty-one times, just modestly smiled.

The lady continued: 'Come on, admit it. You are one.' Then she floored us with a line nobody expected: 'You're the ticket tout, aren't you?'

She genuinely had no idea who he was and wanted a late cheap ticket to see Marti.

After the gig, Greg made us all laugh by standing outside the Hydro and shouting: 'Get yir knocked-off *Disney on Ice* tickets here.' Proving he's Still Game right enough . . .

So, can you get dodgy gig tickets from a TV star? On this occasion . . .
NAW!

Jan – March 2022

QUESTION 183
7.1.22

The Cookie Monster from *Sesame Street*'s
real name is Sid. Is this true? Aye or Naw?

Ewen Says: Naw
Twitter Says: Aye 54%; Naw 46%
You Say: **Aye** or **Naw**?

QUESTION 184
10.1.22

In the last thirty years, Scottish players have won more
World Snooker Championships than English players.
Is this true? Aye or Naw?

Ewen Says: Aye
Twitter Says: Aye 47%; Naw 53%
You Say: **Aye** or **Naw**?

QUESTION 185
11.1.22

There are more than 500 varieties of potatoes in the UK. Is this true? Aye or Naw?

Ewen Says: Aye
Twitter Says: Aye 56%; Naw 44%
You Say: **Aye** or **Naw**?

QUESTION 186
12.1.22 – Charlie Brown Day

Charlie Brown's dog Snoopy was originally called 'Sniffy'. Is this true? Aye or Naw?

Ewen Says: Naw
Twitter Says: Aye 23%; Naw 77%
You Say: **Aye** or **Naw**?

QUESTION 187
13.1.22

The sloth is the only mammal that does not fart. Is this true? Aye or Naw?

Ewen Says: Aye
Twitter Says: Aye 47%; Naw 53%
You Say: **Aye** or **Naw**?

QUESTION 188
14.1.22 – 150th anniversary of Greyfriars Bobby passing.

Greyfriars Bobby was a wee mongrel.
Is this true? Aye or Naw?

Ewen Says: Naw
Twitter Says: Aye 56%; Naw 44%
You Say: **Aye** or **Naw**?

QUESTION 189
17.1.22

Jason Donovan's Uncle Steven once reached the Australian Open mixed doubles semi-final. Is this true? Aye or Naw?

Ewen Says: Naw
Twitter Says: Aye 54%; Naw 46%
You Say: **Aye** or **Naw**?

QUESTION 190
18.1.22

Pigs are more intelligent than dogs.
Is this true? Aye or Naw?

Ewen Says: Aye
Twitter Says: Aye 57%; Naw 43%
You Say: **Aye** or **Naw**?

QUESTION 191
19.1.22

Ben Nevis is higher than Mount Rushmore.
Is this true? Aye or Naw?

Ewen Says: Aye
Twitter Says: Aye 68%; Naw 32%
You Say: **Aye** or **Naw**?

QUESTION 192
20.1.22 – Cheese Lovers Day

The French eat more cheese than any other country
in the world. Is this true? Aye or Naw?

Ewen Says: Naw
Twitter Says: Aye 53%; Naw 47%
You Say: **Aye** or **Naw**?

QUESTION 193
21.1.22

The original Hampden Park was opened before the
original Tynecastle stadium. Is this true? Aye or Naw?

Ewen Says: Naw
Twitter Says: Aye 47%; Naw 53%
You Say: **Aye** or **Naw**?

QUESTION 194
24.1.22 – National Peanut Butter Day

Smooth peanut butter is more popular than crunchy in the UK. Is this true? Aye or Naw?

Ewen Says: Naw
Twitter Says: Aye 62%; Naw 38%
You Say: **Aye** or **Naw**?

QUESTION 195
25.1.22

Rabbie Burns had more children than Boris Johnson. Is this true? Aye or Naw?

Ewen Says: Aye
Twitter Says: Aye 66%; Naw 34%
You Say: **Aye** or **Naw**?

QUESTION 196
26.1.22

Australia's capital Canberra is cradled between two mountains. The name 'Canberra' translates to cleavage in Aboriginal languages. Is this true? Aye or Naw?

Ewen Says: Aye
Twitter Says: Aye 57%; Naw 43%
You Say: **Aye** or **Naw**?

QUESTION 197
27.1.22

Australia has the largest herd of wild camels
in the world. Is this true? Aye or Naw?

Ewen Says: Naw
Twitter Says: Aye 54%; Naw 46%
You Say: **Aye** or **Naw**?

QUESTION 198
28.1.22

There are two museums in the world dedicated
to the humble kazoo. Is this true? Aye or Naw?

Ewen Says: Naw
Twitter Says: Aye 55%; Naw 45%
You Say: **Aye** or **Naw**?

QUESTION 199
31.1.22 – National Sprout Day

The sprout is an aphrodisiac. Is this true? Aye or Naw?

Ewen Says: Naw
Twitter Says: Aye 27%; Naw 73%
You Say: **Aye** or **Naw**?

QUESTION 200
1.2.22 – Chinese New Year

Chinese New Year falls on a different date each year.
Is this true? Aye or Naw?

Ewen Says: Aye
Twitter Says: Aye 86%; Naw 14%
You Say: **Aye** or **Naw**?

QUESTION 201
2.2.22

Hedgehogs can swim. Is this true? Aye or Naw?

Ewen Says: Aye
Twitter Says: Aye 56%; Naw 44%
You Say: **Aye** or **Naw**?

QUESTION 202
3.2.22

Annie Lennox was working as a hairdresser when she first
met Dave Stewart. She cut his hair and they eventually
formed Eurythmics. Is this true? Aye or Naw?

Ewen Says: Aye
Twitter Says: Aye 71%; Naw 29%
You Say: **Aye** or **Naw**?

QUESTION 203
4.2.22

Budgies don't pee. Is this true? Aye or Naw?

Ewen Says: Aye
Twitter Says: Aye 38%; Naw 62%
You Say: **Aye** or **Naw**?

QUESTION 204
7.2.22

The average car battery in the UK lasts seven years or more. Is this true? Aye or Naw?

Ewen Says: Aye
Twitter Says: Aye 71%; Naw 29%
You Say: **Aye** or **Naw**?

QUESTION 205
8.2.22

There are more active cruise ships in the world than there are days in the year. Is this true? Aye or Naw?

Ewen Says: Aye
Twitter Says: Aye 84%; Naw 16%
You Say: **Aye** or **Naw**?

QUESTION 206
9.2.22

The average male shoe size in the UK
is a size 10. Is this true? Aye or Naw?

Ewen Says: Naw
Twitter Says: Aye 48%; Naw 52%
You Say: **Aye** or **Naw**?

QUESTION 207
10.2.22

The first waterproof umbrella was invented
in China. Is this true? Aye or Naw?

Ewen Says: Aye
Twitter Says: Aye 43%; Naw 57%
You Say: **Aye** or **Naw**?

QUESTION 208
11.2.22

According to *Rolling Stone* magazine, Jimmy Hendrix is
their No. 1 guitarist of all time. Is this true? Aye or Naw?

Ewen Says: Naw
Twitter Says: Aye 67%; Naw 33%
You Say: **Aye** or **Naw**?

QUESTION 209
21.2.22 – We have a week of Adam and the Ants tickets to give away. So Ewen challenged me to come up with 'ANT' themed questions.

Ants can lift twenty times their body weight. Is this true? Aye or Naw?

Ewen Says: Aye
Twitter Says: Aye 89%; Naw 11%
You Say: **Aye** or **Naw**?

QUESTION 210
22.2.22

My Aunty Jean lives in Rothesay ☺.
Is this true? Aye or Naw?

Ewen Says: Aye
Twitter Says: Aye 69%; Naw 31%
You Say: **Aye** or **Naw**?

QUESTION 211
23.2.22

Ewen's Aunty Donna used to bathe him with a dinosaur sponge. Is this true? Aye or Naw?

Ewen Says: I'm Not Answering That
Twitter Says: Aye 91%; Naw 9%
You Say: **Aye** or **Naw**?

QUESTION 212
24.2.22

Ants have highly functioning lungs.
Is this true? Aye or Naw?

Ewen Says: Aye
Twitter Says: Aye 88%; Naw 12%
You Say: **Aye** or **Naw**?

QUESTION 213
28.2.22

In Italy, the Tooth Fairy has a cat who collects
teeth for her. Is this true? Aye or Naw?

Ewen Says: Aye
Twitter Says: Aye 47%; Naw 53%
You Say: **Aye** or **Naw**?

QUESTION 214
1.3.22 – Pancake Day

The No. 1 pancake topping in the UK is
lemon and sugar. Is this true? Aye or Naw?

Ewen Says: Aye
Twitter Says: Aye 38%; Naw 62%
You Say: **Aye** or **Naw**?

QUESTION 215
2.3.22

More people live in Stirling than Livingston.
Is this true? Aye or Naw?

Ewen Says: Naw
Twitter Says: Aye 45%; Naw 55%
You Say: **Aye** or **Naw**?

QUESTION 216
3.3.22

The average coconut tree produces more than
a hundred coconuts a year. Is this true? Aye or Naw?

Ewen Says: Naw
Twitter Says: Aye 51%; Naw 49%
You Say: **Aye** or **Naw**?

QUESTION 217
4.3.22

Relative to body size, the gorilla is the strongest
animal in the world. Is this true? Aye or Naw?

Ewen Says: Aye
Twitter Says: Aye 38%; Naw 62%
You Say: **Aye** or **Naw**?

QUESTION 218
7.3.22 – Alexander Graham Bell Day

Over 75% of households in the UK still have a landline. Is this true? Aye or Naw?

Ewen Says: Naw
Twitter Says: Aye 63%; Naw 37%
You Say: **Aye** or **Naw**?

QUESTION 219
8.3.22

There are more women than men in the world. Is this true? Aye or Naw?

Ewen Says: Aye
Twitter Says: Aye 72%; Naw 28%
You Say: **Aye** or **Naw**?

QUESTION 220
9.3.22

Sindy was a popular doll before Barbie. Is this true? Aye or Naw?

Ewen Says: Aye
Twitter Says: Aye 77%; Naw 23%
You Say: **Aye** or **Naw**?

QUESTION 221
10.9.22

The UK's most played tune on the bagpipes is 'Auld Lang Syne'. Is this true? Aye or Naw?

Ewen Says: Naw
Twitter Says: Aye 22%; Naw 78%
You Say: **Aye** or **Naw**?

QUESTION 222
11.3.22

The most popular middle name for boys in Scotland is James. Is this true? Aye or Naw?

Ewen Says: Aye
Twitter Says: Aye 64%; Naw 36%
You Say: **Aye** or **Naw**?

QUESTION 223
14.3.22 – National Pi Day

The first three digits of the mathematical constant pi are 3.14. Is this true? Aye or Naw?

Ewen Says: Naw
Twitter Says: Aye 89%; Naw 11%
You Say: **Aye** or **Naw**?

QUESTION 224
15.3.22 –The Ides of March

Caesar died before he was fifty years old.
Is this true? Aye or Naw?

Ewen Says: Aye
Twitter Says: Aye 75%; Naw 25%
You Say: **Aye** or **Naw**?

QUESTION 225
16.3.22

Pandas spend over fifteen hours a day sleeping.
Is this true? Aye or Naw?

Ewen Says: Aye
Twitter Says: Aye 86%; Naw 14%
You Say: **Aye** or **Naw**?

QUESTION 226
17.3.22 – St Patrick's Day

Tennent's lager was commercially produced
before Guinness. Is this true? Aye or Naw?

Ewen Says: Aye
Twitter Says: Aye 47%; Naw 53%
You Say: **Aye** or **Naw**?

QUESTION 227
18.3.22 – National Sleep Day

Over 70% of people sleep on their sides.
Is this true? Aye or Naw?

Ewen Says: Naw
Twitter Says: Aye 92%; Naw 8%
You Say: **Aye** or **Naw**?

QUESTION 228
28.3.22

Cats have eighteen toes. Is this true? Aye or Naw?

Ewen Says: Naw
Twitter Says: Aye 33%; Naw 67%
You Say: **Aye** or **Naw**?

QUESTION 229
29.3.22 – World Piano Day

A grand piano has more keys than a standard
upright piano. Is this true? Aye or Naw?

Ewen Says: Naw
Twitter Says: Aye 47%; Naw 53%
You Say: **Aye** or **Naw**?

QUESTION 230
30.3.22

Pop-a-point pencils were invented in the 1960s.
Is this true? Aye or Naw?

Ewen Says: Aye
Twitter Says: Aye 58%; Naw 42%
You Say: **Aye** or **Naw**?

QUESTION 231
31.3.22 – National Crayon Day

By the age of ten, the average child has used over
one thousand crayons. Is this true? Aye or Naw?

Ewen Says: Aye
Twitter Says: Aye 33%; Naw 67%
You Say: **Aye** or **Naw**?

You're playing a blinder! For answers on potatoes, sloths, Jason Donovan, peanut butter, camels, kazoos and sexy sprouts **turn to page 240**.

Do You Ken Ken?

Aye or Naw?

I remember the moment clear as day. Ewen, Producer Cat and I were sitting in a meeting room when our boss/pal Producer Michael said: 'I've got a wee bit of news for you.'

Usually this means he's secured some great tickets for us to give away on the show or something.

'Ken Bruce is joining the line-up and he will be on after you guys.'

It's kind of like playing for Partick Thistle and finding out Messi wants to join.

I'd never met Ken before but he's an absolute icon in the radio industry. Not only was his Radio 2 show with his famous music quiz 'Popmaster' the most listened-to show in the UK, it was the biggest radio show in all of Europe.

Changing to Greatest Hits Radio was a big move for us. Suddenly we became Scotland's first national commercial radio station. Signing Ken was massive.

Our bosses decided to roll out the red carpet for Ken's first visit to the studios. The entire line-up was brought together in the reception area waiting for him. Andy Crane, Jackie

Brambles, Jenny Powell, Paul Gambaccini and Kate Thornton to name but a few.

There were party poppers, party hats, scantily clad acrobats and a Mexican mariachi band. Ken arrived and looked delighted and mortified in equal measure. Our bosses wanted to take us all out for a swanky celebratory lunch, but Ken quietly suggested a visit to the local pub instead.

This is when I knew he was a proper legend.

Instead of a sit-down formal meal, he had one pint of Guinness and did the rounds saying hello to everyone and making sure he knew exactly who we were and what we did.

My lunch that day was two bags of scampi fries and more mini-Proseccos than I care to remember. I feel that Jackie Brambles and I could be quite a team on a night out.

A lovely end to an exciting day. Ewen and I are both terrible at Popmaster; however, we are enjoying working with Ken, who not only brings years of professionalism to our chaos but takes us to the pub too . . .

So, do we ken Ken?
Aye . . . now we do . . .

April – June 2022

QUESTION 232
1.4.22 – April Fool's Day

Ancient Romans had their own version of April
Fool's Day called 'Poopis Hillaria', where they left
small fake mud poops on their friend's doorstep.
Is this true? Aye or Naw?

Ewen Says: Naw
Twitter Says: Aye 22%; Naw 78%
You Say: **Aye** or **Naw**?

QUESTION 233
4.4.22

Purple carrots are healthier than orange carrots.
Is this true? Aye or Naw?

Ewen Says: Naw
Twitter Says: Aye 26%; Naw 74%
You Say: **Aye** or **Naw**?

5.4.22 – National Caramel Day

Tunnock's make and sell over 5 million Caramel Wafers every week. Is this true? Aye or Naw?

Ewen Says: Aye
Twitter Says: Aye 47%; Naw 53%
You Say: **Aye** or **Naw**?

QUESTION 235
6.4.22

Burberry is an officially recognised tartan. Is this true? Aye or Naw?

Ewen Says: Naw
Twitter Says: Aye 26%; Naw 74%
You Say: **Aye** or **Naw**?

QUESTION 236
8.4.22

Edinburgh was the first zoo in the world to successfully breed penguins. Is this true? Aye or Naw?

Ewen Says: Aye
Twitter Says: Aye 62%; Naw 38%
You Say: **Aye** or **Naw**?

QUESTION 237
19.4.22

The average person eats more than 5lb of garlic a year. Is this true? Aye or Naw?

Ewen Says: Aye
Twitter Says: Aye 37%; Naw 63%
You Say: **Aye** or **Naw**?

QUESTION 238
20.4.22

The most popular milkshake flavour of students in the UK is banana. Is this true? Aye or Naw?

Ewen Says: Naw
Twitter Says: Aye 31%; Naw 69%
You Say: **Aye** or **Naw**?

QUESTION 239
21.4.22 – National Tea Day

Tetley's tea is the most popular tea in Scotland. Is this true? Aye or Naw?

Ewen Says: Aye
Twitter Says: Aye 58%; Naw 42%
You Say: **Aye** or **Naw**?

QUESTION 240
22.4.22

Pigs cannot see the sky. Is this true? Aye or Naw?

Ewen Says: Aye
Twitter Says: Aye 47%; Naw 53%
You Say: **Aye** or **Naw**?

QUESTION 241
26.4.22

Elon Musk's real name is Kevin.
Is this true? Aye or Naw?

Ewen Says: Aye
Twitter Says: Aye 32%; Naw 68%
You Say: **Aye** or **Naw**?

QUESTION 242
27.4.22 – Storytelling Day

According to *Reader's Digest*, Cinderella is the most
popular fairy tale of all time. Is this true? Aye or Naw?

Ewen Says: Aye
Twitter Says: Aye 47%; Naw 53%
You Say: **Aye** or **Naw**?

QUESTION 243
28.4.22

According to Google, Spider-Man is the most popular superhero in 2022. Is this true? Aye or Naw?

Ewen Says: Aye
Twitter Says: Aye 61%; Naw 39%
You Say: **Aye** or **Naw**?

QUESTION 244
29.4.22

An hour of tap dancing burns more calories than an hour of boxing. Is this true? Aye or Naw?

Ewen Says: Aye
Twitter Says: Aye 67%; Naw 33%
You Say: **Aye** or **Naw**?

QUESTION 245
5.5.22 –National Astronaut Day

There are currently more than twenty people in space. Is this true? Aye or Naw?

Ewen Says: Aye
Twitter Says: Aye 54%; Naw 46%
You Say: **Aye** or **Naw**?

QUESTION 246
10.5.22 – Bono's 62nd birthday

Before finding fame, Bono started an apprenticeship as an electrician. Is this true? Aye or Naw?

Ewen Says: Aye
Twitter Says: Aye 81%; Naw 19%
You Say: **Aye** or **Naw**?

QUESTION 247
11.5.22 –National eat what you want day

Pizza is the most popular food in the world in 2022. Is this true? Aye or Naw?

Ewen Says: Aye
Twitter Says: Aye 61%; Naw 39%
You Say: **Aye** or **Naw**?

QUESTION 248
12.5.22

There are more pigeons than mice in the world. Is this true? Aye or Naw?

Ewen Says: Aye
Twitter Says: Aye 29%; Naw 71%
You Say: **Aye** or **Naw**?

QUESTION 249
13.5.22

There are more cats than dogs in the world.
Is this true? Aye or Naw?

Ewen Says: Aye
Twitter Says: Aye 47%; Naw 53%
You Say: **Aye** or **Naw**?

QUESTION 250
16.5.22

Over 65% of households in the UK own a BBQ.
Is this true? Aye or Naw?

Ewen Says: Naw
Twitter Says: Aye 46%; Naw 54%
You Say: **Aye** or **Naw**?

QUESTION 251
17.5.22

Peanuts are not nuts. Is this true? Aye or Naw?

Ewen Says: Naw
Twitter Says: Aye 44%; Naw 56%
You Say: **Aye** or **Naw**?

QUESTION 252
18.5.22

Spanish teams have won the most Europa League and UEFA cup games. Is this true? Aye or Naw?

Ewen Says: Naw
Twitter Says: Aye 79%; Naw 21%
You Say: **Aye** or **Naw**?

QUESTION 253
19.5.22

There are more accountants than doctors in the UK. Is this true? Aye or Naw?

Ewen Says: Aye
Twitter Says: Aye 82%; Naw 18%
You Say: **Aye** or **Naw**?

QUESTION 254
20.5.22

Pepperoni is the most popular pizza sold in the UK. Is this true? Aye or Naw?

Ewen Says: Aye
Twitter Says: Aye 57%; Naw 43%
You Say: **Aye** or **Naw**?

QUESTION 255
23.5.22 – World Turtle Day

Turtles have teeth. Is this true? Aye or Naw?

Ewen Says: Naw
Twitter Says: Aye 50%; Naw 50%
You Say: **Aye** or **Naw**?

QUESTION 256
24.5.22 – National Brothers Day

Noel Gallagher is more than eight years older than brother Liam. Is this true? Aye or Naw?

Ewen Says: Aye
Twitter Says: Aye 21%; Naw 79%
You Say: **Aye** or **Naw**?

QUESTION 257
25.5.22 – National Wine Day

Red wine is more popular than white wine in Scotland. Is this true? Aye or Naw?

Ewen Says: Aye
Twitter Says: Aye 48%; Naw 52%
You Say: **Aye** or **Naw**?

QUESTION 258
26.5.22

More people live in New York than London.
Is this true? Aye or Naw?

Ewen Says: Aye
Twitter Says: Aye 70%; Naw 30%
You Say: **Aye** or **Naw**?

QUESTION 259
6.6.22 – National Eyewear Day

Over 60% of people in the UK wear glasses or
contact lenses. Is this true? Aye or Naw?

Ewen Says: Aye
Twitter Says: Aye 78%; Naw 22%
You Say: **Aye** or **Naw**?

QUESTION 260
7.6.22

Green eyes are the second most common eye
colour in the UK. Is this true? Aye or Naw?

Ewen Says: Naw
Twitter Says: Aye 23%; Naw 77%
You Say: **Aye** or **Naw**?

QUESTION 261
8.6.22 – Armenia v Scotland

Chess is a mandatory subject for primary school kids in Armenia. Is this true? Aye or Naw?

Ewen Says: Naw
Twitter Says: Aye 68%; Naw 32%
You Say: **Aye** or **Naw**?

QUESTION 262
9.6.22 – National Birds and Bees Day

In its lifetime, one bee can make two jars of honey. Is this true? Aye or Naw?

Ewen Says: Aye
Twitter Says: Aye 60%; Naw 40%
You Say: **Aye** or **Naw**?

QUESTION 263
10.6.22

Over 80% of birds do not have penises. Is this true? Aye or Naw?

Ewen Says: Aye
Twitter Says: Aye 58%; Naw 42%
You Say: **Aye** or **Naw**?

QUESTION 264

13.6.22 – We have more Adam and the Ants tickets to give away, so Ewen challenged me to create another week of ANT questions.

There are over 12,000 species of ants in the world.
Is this true? Aye or Naw?

Ewen Says: Naw
Twitter Says: Aye 55%; Naw 45%
You Say: **Aye** or **Naw**?

QUESTION 265
14.6.22

Adam Ant was born in Antigua. Is this true? Aye or Naw?

Ewen Says: Aye
Twitter Says: Aye 34%; Naw 66%
You Say: **Aye** or **Naw**?

QUESTION 266
15.6.22

'Stand and Deliver' was Adam and the Ants first No. 1 song. Is this true? Aye or Naw?

Ewen Says: Aye
Twitter Says: Aye 50%; Naw 50%
You Say: **Aye** or **Naw**?

QUESTION 267
16.6.22

In *The Wizard of Oz*, Dorothy lived with her
Aunt Dee. Is this true? Aye or Naw?

Ewen Says: Naw
Twitter Says: Aye 28%; Naw 72%
You Say: **Aye** or **Naw**?

QUESTION 268
17.6.22

Ant is older than Dec. Is this true? Aye or Naw?

Ewen Says: Aye
Twitter Says: Aye 50%; Naw 50%
You Say: **Aye** or **Naw**?

QUESTION 269
20.6.22

There are more Starbucks than McDonald's
in Scotland. Is this true? Aye or Naw?

Ewen Says: Naw
Twitter Says: Aye 38%; Naw 62%
You Say: **Aye** or **Naw**?

QUESTION 270
21.6.22 – Summer Solstice

The Callanish standing stones in Lewis are older than Stonehenge. Is this true? Aye or Naw?

Ewen Says: Naw
Twitter Says: Aye 80%; Naw 20%
You Say: **Aye** or **Naw**?

QUESTION 271
22.6.22 – The Eagles play Murrayfield

Eagles eat monkeys. Is this true? Aye or Naw?

Ewen Says: Aye
Twitter Says: Aye 59%; Naw 41%
You Say: **Aye** or **Naw**?

QUESTION 272
23.6.22 – The Royal Highland Show opens

The Royal Highland Show will be home to over 10,000 animals this week. Is this true? Aye or Naw?

Ewen Says: Aye
Twitter Says: Aye 72%; Naw 28%
You Say: **Aye** or **Naw**?

QUESTION 273
24.6.22 – Take Your Dog to Work Day

Greyhounds can run faster than wild cheetahs.
Is this true? Aye or Naw?

Ewen Says: Aye
Twitter Says: Aye 16%; Naw 84%
You Say: **Aye** or **Naw**?

QUESTION 274
27.6.22 – National Bingo Day

More people play bingo than football.
Is this true? Aye or Naw?

Ewen Says: Naw

Twitter Says:
Aye 57%; Naw 43%

You Say:
Aye or **Naw**?

QUESTION 275
28.6.22

Tennis is the most popular individual sport
in the world. Is this true? Aye or Naw?

Ewen Says: Aye
Twitter Says: Aye 26%; Naw 74%
You Say: **Aye** or **Naw**?

QUESTION 276
29.6.22 – National Fisherman Day

Some fish can walk. Is this true? Aye or Naw?

Ewen Says: Aye
Twitter Says: Aye 61%; Naw 39%
You Say: **Aye** or **Naw**?

QUESTION 277
30.6.22

YouTube has more monthly users than Facebook.
Is this true? Aye or Naw?

Ewen Says: Aye
Twitter Says: Aye 71%; Naw 29%
You Say: **Aye** or **Naw**?

To find out if you were correct about pigs, wine, accountants, turtles (more turtles? – I must really like turtles!) and
Noel Gallagher, **turn to page 244.**

Fish Is Always Good for You?

Aye or Naw?

Here's a fishy story with a valuable lesson attached.

Let me introduce you to Jim the Fishman, Andrew and Young Finlay. They work in the Marc Horsburgh Fish Merchants shed in St Monans in Fife gutting haddock every day.

They have our show on every morning and are regular contributors getting in touch with song requests, answers to 'Aye or Naw' or just to say hello.

Their most memorable message ever said: 'Please say hello to Young Finlay, he's just come to work straight from the airport after his first ever boys' holiday to Kavos and he's in bits.'

Now working with a hangover is never good, but gutting fish after a wild trip, a long flight and no sleep is a new level of pain. Out of genuine concern, I asked Jim the Fishman how our young adventurer was faring elbow deep in stinky fish guts.

The reply had everyone in the studio crying with laughter. They sent a photo. It was misery personified. Pain, regret, hilarious! Our bold hero was dressed in his orange work overalls, hair dishevelled, eyes red and skin a curious mix of lemon yellow and luminous green.

So vivid was this snap of shame, we secretly used it as the group picture on our Breakfast Show WhatsApp group for months. (We eventually told them, and he was well chuffed!)

I've included his picture in this book, a reminder to us all about the evils of drink and a valuable lesson – don't gut fish after a five-day bender!

So, is fish always good for you?
NAW!!!!

July – Sept 2022

QUESTION 278
1.7.22 – Canada Day

Beavers' teeth are orange. Is this true? Aye or Naw?

Ewen Says: Aye
Twitter Says: Aye 41%; Naw 59%
You Say: **Aye** or **Naw**?

QUESTION 279
4.7.22

Alice in Wonderland is based on real life.
Is this true? Aye or Naw?

Ewen Says: Aye
Twitter Says: Aye 47%; Naw 53%
You Say: **Aye** or **Naw**?

QUESTION 280
5.7.22

Cows can only dream if they are lying down.
Is this true? Aye or Naw?

Ewen Says: Aye
Twitter Says: Aye 35%; Naw 65%
You Say: **Aye** or **Naw**?

QUESTION 281
7.7.22 – World Chocolate Day

White chocolate is not chocolate.
Is this true? Aye or Naw?

Ewen Says: Aye
Twitter Says: Aye 63%; Naw 37%
You Say: **Aye** or **Naw**?

QUESTION 282
8.7.22 – World Kebab Day

Kebabs were invented in Germany.
Is this true? Aye or Naw?

Ewen Says: Aye
Twitter Says: Aye 62%; Naw 38%
You Say: **Aye** or **Naw**?

QUESTION 283
11.7.22 – National Mojito Day

Mojitos were invented in Mexico.
Is this true? Aye or Naw?

Ewen Says: Aye
Twitter Says: Aye 41%; Naw 59%
You Say: **Aye** or **Naw**?

QUESTION 284
12.7.22 – National Cow Appreciation Day

A cow has fewer than twenty teeth.
Is this true? Aye or Naw?

Ewen Says: Aye
Twitter Says: Aye 71%; Naw 29%
You Say: **Aye** or **Naw**?

QUESTION 285
13.7.22 – National French Fries Day

French Fries originated in France.
Is this true? Aye or Naw?

Ewen Says: Naw
Twitter Says: Aye 8%; Naw 92%
You Say: **Aye** or **Naw**?

QUESTION 286
14.7.22 – National Nude Day

You are legally allowed to be naked everywhere
in the UK. Is this true? Aye or Naw?

Ewen Says: Naw
Twitter Says: Aye 16%; Naw 84%
You Say: **Aye** or **Naw**?

QUESTION 287
15.7.22 – I Love Horses Day

Horses only breathe through their nostrils.
Is this true? Aye or Naw?

Ewen Says: Naw
Twitter Says: Aye 64%; Naw 36%
You Say: **Aye** or **Naw**?

QUESTION 288
18.7.22

Fewer than 4% of homes in the UK have
air conditioning. Is this true? Aye or Naw?

Ewen Says: Naw
Twitter Says: Aye 96%; Naw 4%
You Say: **Aye** or **Naw**?

QUESTION 289
19.7.22

The daquiri was invented in Cuba.
Is this true? Aye or Naw?

Ewen Says: Naw
Twitter Says: Aye 55%; Naw 45%
You Say: **Aye** or **Naw**?

Our new shiny profile pictures looking sensible after being told by the big bosses that we 'muck about too much' in photos.

Ewen and Cat – proving the bosses were right!

No Marti no party! Always fun when my first love joins the show.

'Love is all Around'. Backstage at the Usher Hall in Marti's dressing room. Scene of the Teacake crime.

Cat's Out the Bag – My second book became an Amazon bestseller raising over £100,000 for Cash for Kids. Thank You.

Edinburgh Fringe frolics with Randy Feltface. Nothing says the festival more than winching a boggly-eyed purple puppet.

The three amigos. My radio partners in nonsense, Arlene from Forth 1 and Wee Vixen.

Rewind Festival. Rocking the
eighties big hair at Scone Palace.

Ewen thinks he is Maverick from
Top Gun – the hat says it all.

Claire Grogan from Altered Images making
Ewen's teenage dreams come true.

NO COMMENT!

Girls on film. Well, a big stage really. Arlene and I unexpectedly opening for Duran Duran!

What's the story? *Balamory* of course! Celebrating 20 years of *Balamory* with PC Plum and Miss Hoolie.

What a night out this could have been! Festival fun with Jason Byrne, John Bishop, Amy Macdonald and Richard Foster.

River City turns twenty. Gayle Telfer Stevens, who plays Caitlin, gives us the tour.

Behind the scenes with Stephen Purdon, Jordan Young and Scott Fletcher.

Boooo – he's a right bad yin! Soap baddie Lenny and wife Lydia Murdoch, played by Frank Gallagher and Jacqueline Leonard.

Trying to be a 'Mysterious Girl' – with Peter Andre at the Cash for Kids lunch in Glasgow.

When will I, will I have a hottie like this? Matt Goss proving to be the perfect podcast guest.

Above: 'Girls Just Wanna Have Fun'. My new Prosecco crew on Greatest Hits Radio, Jackie Brambles, Jenny Powell and Kate Thornton.

Left: 'I Owe You Nothing'. Well probably quite a lot actually, as Matt Goss paid for all the drinks at his Usher Hall afterparty. Ewen stayed out until 4 a.m.!

Boogie on the Boat – school disco themed party night. Naughty behaviour and detention for everyone on board!

Bowie on the Bus. Sweaty times as Mr Stay Puff on Cash for Kids Day with George, Cassi and producer John, the Clyde 1 breakfast team, plus Ali and Michael from West FM.

A night TOUT with Greg Hemphill. Once you read the story it will make sense!

We ken KEN. Team Greatest Hits Radio Scotland welcoming Ken Bruce, the Popmaster himself, to our new line up.

A fishy tale . . . poor Finlay.

Right: On our way from misery to happiness hanging out with The Proclaimers.

Below: Two Cats are better than one. Loving life with my wee mini-me Producer Cat.

Best pals? Aye or Naw? – Despite the fact he is annoying . . . AYE!

QUESTION 290
20.7.22 –National Lollipop Day

The inspiration for the name 'lollipop' came from the inventor's dog. Is this true? Aye or Naw?

Ewen Says: Aye
Twitter Says: Aye 36%; Naw 64%
You Say: **Aye** or **Naw**?

QUESTION 291
21.7.22 – National Junk Food Day

The average person in the UK will eat more pizzas than burgers in their life. Is this true? Aye or Naw?

Ewen Says: Aye
Twitter Says: Aye 63%; Naw 37%
You Say: **Aye** or **Naw**?

QUESTION 292
22.7.22 – National Mango Day

The mango is the national fruit of five countries.
Is this true? Aye or Naw?

Ewen Says: Aye
Twitter Says: Aye 50%; Naw 50%
You Say: **Aye** or **Naw**?

QUESTION 293
2.8.22 – National Night Out Day (whit?!)

According to new research, the best place to go out
drinking in the UK is Glasgow. Is this true? Aye or Naw?

Ewen Says: Naw
Twitter Says: Aye 56%; Naw 44%
You Say: **Aye** or **Naw**?

QUESTION 294
3.8.22 –National Grab Some Nuts Day. (STOP SNIGGERING, YOU NAUGHTY LOT)

Almonds are the most widely consumed nuts
in the world. Is this true? Aye or Naw?

Ewen Says: Naw
Twitter Says: Aye 41%; Naw 59%
You Say: **Aye** or **Naw**?

QUESTION 295
4.8.22 – National White Wine Day

France produces more white wine than any other country. Is this true? Aye or Naw?

Ewen Says: Aye
Twitter Says: Aye 37%; Naw 63%
You Say: **Aye** or **Naw**?

QUESTION 296
8.8.22 – International Cat Day

Usain Bolt would beat the average domestic cat over 100m. Is this true? Aye or Naw?

Ewen Says: Naw
Twitter Says: Aye 57%; Naw 43%
You Say: **Aye** or **Naw**?

QUESTION 297
9.8.22

The Eiffel Tower is higher in the summer than in the winter. Is this true? Aye or Naw?

Ewen Says: Aye
Twitter Says: Aye 71%; Naw 29%
You Say: **Aye** or **Naw**?

QUESTION 298
10.8.22 – World Lion Day

All lion cubs are born with spots. Is this true? Aye or Naw?

Ewen Says: Naw
Twitter Says: Aye 45%; Naw 55%
You Say: **Aye** or **Naw**?

QUESTION 299
11.8.22 – We are broadcasting from the Edinburgh Festival.

More people live in Edinburgh than Iceland (the country, not the shop! ☺). Is this true? Aye or Naw?

Ewen Says: Aye
Twitter Says: Aye 69%; Naw 31%
You Say: **Aye** or **Naw**?

QUESTION 300
15.8.22

Lightning is hotter than the sun. Is this true? Aye or Naw?

Ewen Says: Aye
Twitter Says: Aye 47%; Naw 53%
You Say: **Aye** or **Naw**?

QUESTION 301
16.8.22 – National Roller Coaster Day

The first roller coaster debuted in the famous Coney Island amusement park in New York. Is this true? Aye or Naw?

Ewen Says: Naw
Twitter Says: Aye 62%; Naw 38%
You Say: **Aye** or **Naw**?

QUESTION 302
17.8.22 – National Love Your Feet Day

We have more than thirty bones in each foot.
Is this true? Aye or Naw?

Ewen Says: Naw
Twitter Says: Aye 79%; Naw 21%
You Say: **Aye** or **Naw**?

QUESTION 303
18.8.22

Jon Bon Jovi is related to Dean Martin.
Is this true? Aye or Naw?

Ewen Says: Aye
Twitter Says: Aye 37%; Naw 63%
You Say: **Aye** or **Naw**?

QUESTION 304
19.8.22 – National Potato Day

China grows more potatoes than any other country.
Is this true? Aye or Naw?

Ewen Says: Naw
Twitter Says: Aye 36%; Naw 64%
You Say: **Aye** or **Naw**?

QUESTION 305
22.8.22

In the film *Toy Story*, Buzz Lightyear was originally meant
to be called 'Lunar Larry'. Is this true? Aye or Naw?

Ewen Says: Aye
Twitter Says: Aye 49%; Naw 51%
You Say: **Aye** or **Naw**?

QUESTION 306
23.8.22

Jurassic Park was the highest grossing film of the 1990s. Is this true? Aye or Naw?

Ewen Says: Naw
Twitter Says: Aye 60%; Naw 40%
You Say: **Aye** or **Naw**?

QUESTION 307
24.8.22 – Coldplay play Hampden

Beyonce is godmother to Chris Martin from Coldplay's son Moses. Is this true? Aye or Naw?

Ewen Says: Naw
Twitter Says: Aye 56%; Naw 44%
You Say: **Aye** or **Naw**?

QUESTION 308
25.8.22

Coldplay are in the top five of highest earning worldwide music tours for 2022. Is this true? Aye or Naw?

Ewen Says: Naw
Twitter Says: Aye 80%; Naw 20%
You Say: **Aye** or **Naw**?

QUESTION 309
26.8.22 – National Toilet Paper Day

Only 30% or less of the world population uses toilet paper. Is this true? Aye or Naw?

Ewen Says: Aye
Twitter Says: Aye 71%; Naw 29%
You Say: **Aye** or **Naw**?

QUESTION 310
29.9.22

The world high jump record is over 8ft. Is this true? Aye or Naw?

Ewen Says: Naw
Twitter Says: Aye 49%; Naw 51%
You Say: **Aye** or **Naw**

QUESTION 311
1.9.22 – Ginger Cat Day

Over 75% of ginger cats are male. Is this true? Aye or Naw?

Ewen Says: Naw
Twitter Says: Aye 31%; Naw 69%
You Say: **Aye** or **Naw**?

QUESTION 312
2.9.22 – World Coconut Day

Coconut water can be used as a substitute for blood.
Is this true? Aye or Naw?

Ewen Says: Naw
Twitter Says: Aye 17%; Naw 83%
You Say: **Aye** or **Naw**?

QUESTION 313
5.9.22 – Freddie Mercury born on this day in 1946

Freddie Mercury was a champion boxer.
Is this true? Aye or Naw?

Ewen Says: Aye
Twitter Says: Aye 46%; Naw 54%
You Say: **Aye** or **Naw**?

QUESTION 314
6.9.22

Seagulls are promiscuous. Is this true? Aye or Naw?

Ewen Says: Naw
Twitter Says: Aye 63%; Naw 37%
You Say: **Aye** or **Naw**?

QUESTION 315
7.9.22 – National Salami Day

The word salami comes from the Latin word 'salare', which means desirable meat. Is this true? Aye or Naw?

Ewen Says: Aye
Twitter Says: Aye 38%; Naw 62%
You Say: **Aye** or **Naw**?

QUESTION 316
8.9.22 – Star Trek Day

There are more episodes of *Star Trek* than *Dr Who*. Is this true? Aye or Naw?

Ewen Says: Aye
Twitter Says: Aye 53%; Naw 47%
You Say: **Aye** or **Naw**?

QUESTION 317
12.9.22 – National Video Game Day

Grand Theft Auto is the bestselling video game of all time. Is this true? Aye or Naw?

Ewen Says: Aye
Twitter Says: Aye 61%; Naw 39%
You Say: **Aye** or **Naw**?

QUESTION 318
13.9.22 – International Chocolate Day

Cadbury's Dairy Milk is the bestselling chocolate bar in the UK. Is this true? Aye or Naw?

Ewen Says: Aye
Twitter Says: Aye 80%; Naw 20%
You Say: **Aye** or **Naw**?

QUESTION 319
14.9.22

The average man in the UK owns more than ten pairs of shoes (including trainers). Is this true? Aye or Naw?

Ewen Says: Aye
Twitter Says: Aye 47%; Naw 53%
You Say: **Aye** or **Naw**?

QUESTION 320
15.9.22 – Make a Hat Day

Over 50 million baseball caps are sold worldwide every year. Is this true? Aye or Naw?

Ewen Says: Aye
Twitter Says: Aye 86%; Naw 14%
You Say: **Aye** or **Naw**?

QUESTION 321
16.9.22 – National Guacamole Day

The name guacamole comes from Aztec words meaning over-ripe avocado. Is this true? Aye or Naw?

Ewen Says: Aye
Twitter Says: Aye 41%; Naw 59%
You Say: **Aye** or **Naw**?

QUESTION 322
20.9.22

The Giant Squid has the largest eyes in the world. Is this true? Aye or Naw?

Ewen Says: Aye
Twitter Says: Aye 51%; Naw 49%
You Say: **Aye** or **Naw**?

QUESTION 323
21.9.22 – Mini Golf Day

Mini golf was first invented in Scotland. Is this true? Aye or Naw?

Ewen Says: Naw
Twitter Says: Aye 30%; Naw 70%
You Say: **Aye** or **Naw**?

QUESTION 324
22.9.22

Elephants can't jump. Is this true? Aye or Naw?

Ewen Says: Aye
Twitter Says: Aye 61%; Naw 39%
You Say: **Aye** or **Naw**?

QUESTION 325
23.9.22

There are more than 280 Munros in Scotland. Is this true? Aye or Naw?

Ewen Says: Naw
Twitter Says: Aye 79%; Naw 21 %
You Say: **Aye** or **Naw**?

QUESTION 326
26.9.22 – Alpaca Day

Alpacas can run faster than 40mph. Is this true? Aye or Naw?

Ewen Says: Naw
Twitter Says: Aye 41%; Naw 59%
You Say: **Aye** or **Naw**?

QUESTION 327
27.9.22 – National Chocolate Milkshake Day

Milkshakes originally contained whisky.
Is this true? Aye or Naw?

Ewen Says: Aye
Twitter Says: Aye 35%; Naw 65%
You Say: **Aye** or **Naw**?

QUESTION 328
28.9.22 – Ask a Stupid Question Day

'What is the time?' is the most Googled question
in the world. Is this true? Aye or Naw?

Ewen Says: Aye
Twitter Says: Aye 39%; Naw 61%
You Say: **Aye** or **Naw**?

QUESTION 329
29.9.22 – International Coffee Day

In the UK people are now drinking more cups of coffee
a day than cups of tea. Is this true? Aye or Naw?

Ewen Says: Aye
Twitter Says: Aye 67%; Naw 33%
You Say: **Aye** or **Naw**?

QUESTION 330
30.9.22

There are ten or more parts of the human body that are three letters long. Is this true? Aye or Naw?

Ewen Says: Aye
Twitter Says: Aye 71%; Naw 29%
You Say: **Aye** or **Naw**?

Still with me? Good on you. To find out if you were right about Buzz Lightyear, kebabs, nudity, giant squid and mini golf **turn to page 247.** I am giving you quite the education!

Did The Proclaimers Walk 500 Miles?

Aye or Naw?

We always love it when Craig and Charlie Reid AKA 'The Proclaimers' come on our show.

Not only are they Scottish songwriting and performing legends, they can wind up Ewen better than anyone else in the world. Their Hibs v Hearts banter is never far from the agenda and fair play to them, they can certainly take it just as much as they dish it out.

They've always been up for a laugh and even helped us out one April Fool's Day years ago on Real Radio when they agreed to pretend that they were a manufactured pop band and not even related. We even got a call from the newspapers about that one!

This time we had arranged a big interview with them ahead of their new album *Dentures Out* and forthcoming tour, in our Edinburgh studios in the St James Quarter. Charlie arrived forty-five minutes ahead of schedule and was full of apologies.

He said: 'My bus was early, because we had more green lights than normal.'

Ewen and I just looked at each other. A Proclaimer. On a bus?

They've sold more than 1,695,000 albums all over the world and could afford a fleet of drivers in luxury limousines, yet Charlie gets the bus?

He laughed at our surprise: 'Oh aye, I got my bus pass when I turned sixty and it's an excellent service to get into the town. When the two of us are not together and I don't have my glasses on nobody has a clue who I am.'

So, did The Proclaimers walk 500 miles?
NAW they took a Lothian bus!

Oct – Dec 2022

QUESTION 331
3.10.22

In the animal kingdom, the fingerprints of gorillas are the closest to humans. Is this true? Aye or Naw?

Ewen Says: Naw
Twitter Says: Aye 71%; Naw 29%
You Say: **Aye** or **Naw**?

QUESTION 332
4.10.22

A litre of water weighs more than a litre of vodka. Is this true? Aye or Naw?

Ewen Says: Naw
Twitter Says: Aye 30%; Naw 70%
You Say: **Aye** or **Naw**?

QUESTION 333
5.10.22

Bananas are radioactive. Is this true? Aye or Naw?

Ewen Says: Aye
Twitter Says: Aye 68%; Naw 32%
You Say: **Aye** or **Naw**?

QUESTION 334
6.10.22

More instant noodles are eaten in India
than Japan. Is this true? Aye or Naw?

Ewen Says: Aye
Twitter Says: Aye 13%; Naw 87%
You Say: **Aye** or **Naw**?

QUESTION 335
7.10.22

Bert and Ernie from *Sesame Street* were named
after characters in the film *Breakfast at Tiffany's*.
Is this true? Aye or Naw?

Ewen Says: Aye
Twitter Says: Aye 51%; Naw 49%
You Say: **Aye** or **Naw**?

QUESTION 336
19.10.22

There is a species of ant in Manhattan called the 'Manhattant'. Is this true? Aye or Naw?

Ewen Says: Naw
Twitter Says: Aye 25%; Naw 75%
You Say: **Aye** or **Naw**?

QUESTION 337
20.10.22 – International Sloth Day

Sloths can poop half their body weight in one go. Is this true? Aye or Naw?

Ewen Says: Naw
Twitter Says: Aye 67%; Naw 33%
You Say: **Aye** or **Naw**?

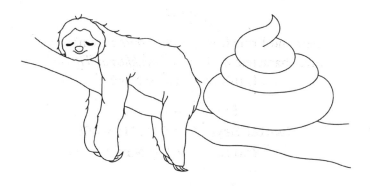

QUESTION 338
21.10.22

In Victorian times people sitting for photos said
'prunes', not 'cheese'. This was to look important
in the pictures. Is this true? Aye or Naw?

Ewen Says: Aye
Twitter Says: Aye 53%; Naw 47%
You Say: **Aye** or **Naw**?

QUESTION 339
24.10.22

There are more trees on the planet than stars
in the solar system. Is this true? Aye or Naw?

Ewen Says: Naw
Twitter Says: Aye 22 %; Naw 78%
You Say: **Aye** or **Naw**?

QUESTION 340
25.10.22

The biggest pyramid in the world is in Egypt.
Is this true? Aye or Naw?

Ewen Says: Naw
Twitter Says: Aye 37%; Naw 63%
You Say: **Aye** or **Naw**?

QUESTION 341
26.10.22

People in the UK will spend more than £700 million on Halloween this year. Is this true? Aye or Naw?

Ewen Says: Aye
Twitter Says: Aye 71%; Naw 29%
You Say: **Aye** or **Naw**?

QUESTION 342
27.10.22

Before joining Take That, Robbie Williams was a double-glazing salesman. Is this true? Aye or Naw?

Ewen Says: Naw
Twitter Says: Aye 41%; Naw 59%
You Say: **Aye** or **Naw**?

QUESTION 343
28.10.22

Frankenstein's monster is called 'Kristov'. Is this true? Aye or Naw?

Ewen Says: Aye
Twitter Says: Aye 48%; Naw 52%
You Say: **Aye** or **Naw**?

QUESTION 344
31.10.22

People in Edinburgh are more likely to claim to see a ghost than anywhere else in the UK. Is this true? Aye or Naw?

Ewen Says: Aye
Twitter Says: Aye 75%; Naw 25%
You Say: **Aye** or **Naw**?

QUESTION 345
1.11.22 – National Calzone Day

Calzone pizzas were invented in America.
Is this true? Aye or Naw?

Ewen Says: Naw
Twitter Says: Aye 58%; Naw 42%
You Say: **Aye** or **Naw**?

QUESTION 346
2.11.22

Plants and trees produce more oxygen than seas and oceans. Is this true? Aye or Naw?

Ewen Says: Aye
Twitter Says: Aye 78%; Naw 22%
You Say: **Aye** or **Naw**?

QUESTION 347
3.11.22

There are jellyfish in space. Is this true? Aye or Naw?

Ewen Says: Aye
Twitter Says: Aye 25%; Naw 75%
You Say: **Aye** or **Naw**?

QUESTION 348
4.11.22

According to new research, the most important ingredient in a roast dinner is gravy. Is this true? Aye or Naw?

Ewen Says: Naw
Twitter Says: Aye 69 %; Naw 31%
You Say: **Aye** or **Naw**?

QUESTION 349
7.11.22 – National Keith Day (Yes, really!)

Keith Richards from The Rolling Stones is older than bandmate Mick Jagger. Is this true? Aye or Naw?

Ewen Says: Aye
Twitter Says: Aye 49%; Naw 51%
You Say: **Aye** or **Naw**?

QUESTION 350
8.11.22 – National Cappuccino Day

The highest number of cappuccinos made in one hour by one person is over 400. Is this true? Aye or Naw?

Ewen Says: Naw
Twitter Says: Aye 49%; Naw 51%
You Say: **Aye** or **Naw**?

QUESTION 351
9.11.22 – British Pudding Day

The UK's favourite pudding in 2022 is
sticky toffee pudding. Is this true? Aye or Naw?

Ewen Says: Aye
Twitter Says: Aye 67%; Naw 33%
You Say: **Aye** or **Naw**?

QUESTION 352
10.11.22 – Sesame Street Day

Bert, from Bert and Ernie in *Sesame Street*,
has a twin brother. Is this true? Aye or Naw?

Ewen Says: Aye
Twitter Says: Aye 53%; Naw 47%
You Say: **Aye** or **Naw**?

QUESTION 353
11.11.22 – National Pickle Day

Cleopatra used to regularly eat pickles to keep
her beautiful. Is this true? Aye or Naw?

Ewen Says: Naw
Twitter Says: Aye 58%; Naw 42%
You Say: **Aye** or **Naw**?

QUESTION 354
14.11.22

Westlife have had more UK No. 1's than The Beatles.
Is this true? Aye or Naw?

Ewen Says: Naw
Twitter Says: Aye 55%; Naw 45%
You Say: **Aye** or **Naw**?

QUESTION 355
15.11.22 – National Drummer Day

Dave Grohl from the Foo Fighters and Nirvana
studied law for one year at university before dropping
out to tour with a band. Is this true? Aye or Naw?

Ewen Says: Aye
Twitter Says: Aye 73%; Naw 27%
You Say: **Aye** or **Naw**?

QUESTION 356
16.11.22 – National Clarinet Day

Gloria Estefan is a skilled clarinet player and
linguist and was once offered a job by the C.I.A.
Is this true? Aye or Naw?

Ewen Says: Naw
Twitter Says: Aye 71%; Naw 29%
You Say: **Aye** or **Naw**?

QUESTION 357
17.11.22

Australia is wider than the moon.
Is this true? Aye or Naw?

Ewen Says: Aye
Twitter Says: Aye 36%; Naw 64%
You Say: **Aye** or **Naw**?

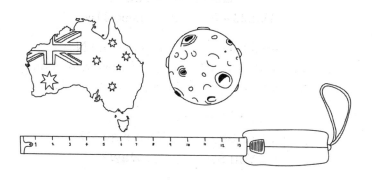

QUESTION 358
18.11.22

Mickey Mouse is older than his girlfriend Minnie.
Is this true? Aye or Naw?

Ewen Says: Naw
Twitter Says: Aye 73%; Naw 23%
You Say: **Aye** or **Naw**?

QUESTION 359
21.11.22

Westlife have had more than double the number of UK No. 1's than Boyzone. Is this true? Aye or Naw?

Ewen Says: Aye
Twitter Says: Aye 74%; Naw 26%
You Say: **Aye** or **Naw**?

QUESTION 360
23.11.22

The A1 is the longest numbered road in the UK. Is this true? Aye or Naw?

Ewen Says: Naw
Twitter Says: Aye 58%; Naw 42%
You Say: **Aye** or **Naw**?

QUESTION 361
24.11.22 – Boyband Week

'Love Me for a Reason' was Boyzone's bestselling single. Is this true? Aye or Naw?

Ewen Says: Naw
Twitter Says: Aye 58%; Naw 42%
You Say: **Aye** or **Naw**?

QUESTION 362
25.11.22 – Boy Band Week

Take That have sold more records than
the Backstreet Boys. Is this true? Aye or Naw?

Ewen Says: Aye
Twitter Says: Aye 56%; Naw 44%
You Say: **Aye** or **Naw**?

QUESTION 363
28.11.22 – World Cup, Brazil v Switzerland

Brazil is the largest country in South America.
Is this true? Aye or Naw?

Ewen Says: Aye
Twitter Says: Aye 68%; Naw 32%
You Say: **Aye** or **Naw**?

QUESTION 364
29.11.22

Rod Stewart's dad was born in Glasgow.
Is this true? Aye or Naw?

Ewen Says: Aye
Twitter Says: Aye 54%; Naw 46%
You Say: **Aye** or **Naw**?

QUESTION 365
1.12.22

There are more than ten miles of fairy lights on the world-famous Rockefeller Christmas Tree in New York.
Is this true? Aye or Naw?

Ewen Says: Naw
Twitter Says: Aye 76%; Naw 24%
You Say: **Aye** or **Naw**?

QUESTION 366
6.12.22 – World Cup – Portugal v Switzerland

The population of Morocco is larger than the population of Portugal and Switzerland combined.
Is this true? Aye or Naw?

Ewen Says: Aye
Twitter Says: Aye 69%; Naw 31%
You Say: **Aye** or **Naw**?

QUESTION 367
7.12.22

Google was originally called 'Brain-rub'.
Is this true? Aye or Naw?

Ewen Says: Aye
Twitter Says: Aye 21%; Naw 79%
You Say: **Aye** or **Naw**?

QUESTION 368
8.12.22

Dogs can be left-pawed or right-pawed, just like humans can be left or right-handed. Is this true? Aye or Paw?

Ewen Says: Aye
Twitter Says: Aye 75 %; Naw 35 %
You Say: **Aye** or **Naw**?

QUESTION 369
9.12.22

Three Scottish footballers have been placed in FIFA's Player of the year or Ballon d'Or since its inception in 1956. Is this true? Aye or Naw?

EWEN Says: Naw
Twitter Says: Aye 61%; Naw 39%
You Say: **Aye** or **Naw**?

QUESTION 370
12.12.22

The snow on Venus is made of metal. Is this true? Aye or Naw?

EWEN Says: Naw
Twitter Says: Aye 37%; Naw 63%
You Say: **Aye** or **Naw**?

QUESTION 371
13.12.22 – World Cup Semi-final – Argentina v Croatia

Argentina has more than twelve times the population of Croatia. Is this true? Aye or Naw?

EWEN Says: Naw
Twitter Says: Aye 37%; Naw 63%
You Say: **Aye** or **Naw**?

QUESTION 372
14.12.22 – World Cup Semi-final – France v Morocco

The current capital of Morocco is Marrakesh. Is this true? Aye or Naw?

EWEN Says: Naw
Twitter Says: Aye 50%; Naw 50%
You Say: **Aye** or **Naw**?

QUESTION 373
15.12.22

The small intestine is longer than the large intestine. Is this true? Aye or Naw?

Ewen Says: Aye
Twitter Says: Aye 77%; Naw 33%
You Say: **Aye** or **Naw**?

QUESTION 374
16.12.22 – Boy band Blue are playing the Hydro tonight

Blue is one of the three original primary colours.
Is this true? Aye or Naw?

EWEN Says: Naw
Twitter Says: Aye 68%; Naw 32%
You Say: **Aye** or **Naw**?

QUESTION 375
20.12.22 – TV legend Jackie Bird is in the studio with us

Only male turkeys gobble. Is this true? Aye or Naw?

EWEN Says: Naw
Twitter Says: Aye 48%; Naw 52%
You Say: **Aye** or **Naw**?

QUESTION 376
21.12.22

Today is the winter solstice. Is this true? Aye or Naw?

EWEN Says: Naw
Twitter Says: Aye 89%; Naw 11%
You Say: **Aye** or **Naw**?

For answers on jellyfish, radioactive bananas, pyramids and ghosts (what a movie that would be!) **turn to page 252.**

When Will Ewen, Will Ewen Be Famous . . . and Can Matt Goss Help?

Aye or Naw?

Ewen's bromance with Matt Goss from eighties boyband Bros was already established when I came back onto the Breakfast Show scene. I can't really explain why, but they both just click. There is a trust, an understanding and a friendship which makes for a curious yet amusing dynamic.

When Matt flew back from his Las Vegas residency to star on Strictly Come Dancing, Ewen was his number one supporter. And when he came into our studio to promote his new tour, I was a bit starstruck because he's so classically handsome and enigmatic in real life.

While he was warming up singing their classic hit 'When Will I Be Famous' I sent a video to my pals from school including Debbie who used to have Smash Hits posters with his face on them all over her bedroom wall.

Matt is a very kind, sensitive soul. After a 'Ewen and Cat – Uncut' podcast with us, he asked everyone apart from me to leave the studio. I hoped he was about to fire in. He wasn't.

However, compassionate love advice was on hand. He held

my hand and said gently: 'Cat, you need to open yourself up to the Universe, you're a beautiful soul, let someone special in.'

At which point Ewen shattered this Zen encounter by rattling the door shouting: 'Are you two at it?'

My favourite moment with Matt happened during his wonderful concert at the Usher Hall in Edinburgh with the Philharmonic Orchestra. In front of a packed house on his final song, he announced: 'Where is my friend Ewen from the Breakfast Show? Get up here.'

I've never seen Ewen so shy. Gingerly he made his way onto the stage, where his role was to be a backing dancer.

You've heard of bad dad dancing; Ewen showcased bad grandad dancing, his stage nerves diminishing in direct correlation to the rapturous cheers! Ewen's confidence returning, the memory of him twerking, grinding and lap dancing Matt's microphone stand will probably haunt those who saw it forever.

Will we ever recover? *'I can't answer, I can't answer that ...'*

So, when will Ewen, will Ewen be famous – and can Matt Goss help?

AYE ... although infamous is maybe closer to the truth!

Jan – March 2023

QUESTION 377
9.1.23 – National Apricot Day

Apricot trees can produce fruit for over fifty years.
Is this true? Aye or Naw?

Ewen Says: Aye
Twitter Says: Aye 73%; Naw 27%
You Say: **Aye** or **Naw**?

QUESTION 378
10.1.23

Frogs can be hypnotised. Is this true? Aye or Naw?

Ewen Says: Naw
Twitter Says: Aye 69%; Naw 31%
You Say: **Aye** or **Naw**?

QUESTION 379
11.2.23

Switzerland is bordered by exactly four countries.
Is this true? Aye or Naw?

Ewen Says: Naw
Twitter Says: Aye 77%; Naw 23%
You Say: **Aye** or **Naw**?

QUESTION 380
12.1.23 – Kiss a Ginger Day

I dedicate this question to my good friend Michelle McManus, Pop Idol winner 2003, who always aspired to this and married Jeff, the nicest ginger of all.

Over 100 million people in the world have ginger hair. Is this true? Aye or Naw?

Ewen Says: Naw

Twitter Says: Aye 54%; Naw 46%

You Say: **Aye** or **Naw**?

QUESTION 381
13.1.23

The letter E is the most commonly used letter in the English language. Is this true? Aye or Naw?

Ewen Says: Aye

Twitter Says: Aye 75%; Naw 25%

You Say: **Aye** or **Naw**? (*If you paid attention earlier in the book you should know this!* ☺)

QUESTION 382
16.1.23

Canada has the longest coastline of any country in the world. Is this true? Aye or Naw?

Ewen Says: Naw

Twitter Says: Aye 59%; Naw 41%

You Say: **Aye** or **Naw**?

QUESTION 383

17.1.23 – National Popeye Day. The cartoon first
appeared in print on this day, but what year?

The cartoon Popeye first appeared in the 1930s.
Is this true? Aye or Naw?

Ewen Says: Naw
Twitter Says: Aye 74% ; Naw 26%
You Say: **Aye** or **Naw**?

QUESTION 384

18.1.23 – Winnie the Pooh Day.
This date is the birthday of Winnie the Pooh author A.A.Milne.

Winnie the Pooh was based on a real-life bear.
Is this true? Aye or Naw?

Ewen Says: Naw
Twitter Says: Aye 50%; Naw-50%
You Say: **Aye** or **Naw**?

QUESTION 385

20.1.23 – What cheese says hello to you. Halloumi.
Hallo-me. Oh, come on, it's not bad!

Halloumi is now the second most popular cheese
in the UK. Is this true? Aye or Naw?

Ewen Says: Aye
Twitter Says: Aye 37% ; Naw 63%
You Say: **Aye** or **Naw**?

QUESTION 386

23.1.23 – Matt Goss from Bros is in our studio this morning. They famously put Grolsch bottle tops on their Doc Martin boots in a quirky eighties fashion statement that still makes no sense.

Grolsch Lager is brewed in Germany.
Is this true ? Aye or Naw?

Ewen Says: Aye
Twitter Says: Aye 51% ; Naw 49%
You Say: **Aye** or **Naw**?

QUESTION 387
24.1.23 – National Pie Day

The most popular savoury pie in the UK is steak pie. Is this true? Aye or Naw?

Ewen Says: Aye
Twitter Says: Aye 66%; Naw 34%
You Say: **Aye** or **Naw**?

QUESTION 388
25.1.23 – Burns Day

Rabbie Burns was the first person to appear on a Coca-Cola bottle. Is this true? Aye or Naw?

Ewen Says: Aye
Twitter Says: Aye 23% ; Naw 77%
You Say: **Aye** or **Naw**?

QUESTION 389
26.1.23

Today we revealed the Rewind line-up for 2023, and Erasure are headlining. They are one of Ewen's favourite bands. He loves Andy Bell. He once chased him down the platform of a Tube station in London shouting 'Andy I love you'. I know this happened because I was there. Andy looked scared and whispered 'thanks' before deliberately getting on a different carriage to us.

Ewen claims to know EVERYTHING about Andy Bell.

Erasure singer Andy Bell used to sell shoes before he was famous. Is this true? Aye or Naw?

Ewen Says: Naw
Twitter Says: Aye 84%; Naw 16%
You Say: **Aye** or **Naw**?

QUESTION 390
27.1.23 – National Chocolate Cake Day

Chocolate cake is the third most popular cake in the UK. Is this true? Aye or Naw?

Ewen Says: Naw
Twitter Says: Aye 47%; Naw 53%
You Say: **Aye** or **Naw**?

QUESTION 391
30.1.23 – Bubble Wrap Appreciation Day

Bubble wrap was originally invented as wallpaper.
Is this true? Aye or Naw?

Ewen Says: Naw
Twitter Says: Aye 30%; Naw 70%
You Say: **Aye** or **Naw**?

QUESTION 392
31.1.23 – Justin Timberlake's 41st birthday.

Justin Timberlake's real name is James Timberland.
Is this true? Aye or Naw?

Ewen Says: Aye
Twitter Says: Aye 15%; Naw 85%
You Say: **Aye** or **Naw**?

QUESTION 393
1.2.23

According to Cybernews, the most popular password in
the world in 2023 is 123456. Is this true? Aye or Naw?

Ewen Says: Naw
Twitter Says: Aye 35%; Naw 64%
You Say: **Aye** or **Naw**?

QUESTION 394

2.2.23 – Hearts played Rangers in a Scottish Cup tie last night. Ewen asked for a Hearts question today! Hearts lost 3–0 at home. Ewen wants to hide in a cave.

The nickname 'Jambos' for Hearts' fans originated because Tynecastle stadium was built next to a successful jam factory in 1886.

Ewen Says: Naw
Twitter Says: Aye 38%; Naw 62%
You Say: **Aye** or **Naw**?

QUESTION 395

3.3.23 – National Golden Retriever Day

There are more golden retrievers than sausage dogs (dachshunds) in the UK. Is this true? Aye or Naw?

Ewen Says: Naw
Twitter Says: Aye 87%; Naw 13%
You Say: **Aye** or **Naw**?

QUESTION 396

6.2.23 – Chopsticks Day

Over 40% of the world's population uses chopsticks on a daily basis. Is this true? Aye or Naw?

Ewen Says: Aye
Twitter Says: Aye 51%; Naw 49%
You Say: **Aye** or **Naw**?

QUESTION 397
7.2.23 – National Ballet Day

Ballet was first performed in Italy.
Is this true? Aye or Naw?

Ewen Says: Naw
Twitter Says: Aye 32%; Naw 68%
You Say: **Aye** or **Naw**?

QUESTION 398
8.2.23 – Fly a Kite Day

Kites were first invented and flown in Japan.
Is this true? Aye or Naw?

Ewen Says: Aye
Twitter Says: Aye 48%; Naw 52%
You Say: **Aye** or **Naw**?

QUESTION 399
9.2.23 – Chocolate Day

Dairy Milk is the UK's longest running chocolate bar.
(A bar invented years ago still on sale today.)
Is this true? Aye or Naw?

Ewen Says: Naw
Twitter Says : Aye 60%; Naw 40%
You Say: **Aye** or **Naw**?

QUESTION 400
20.2.23

Glaswegians swear more than people from any other city in the UK. Is this true? Aye or ******* Naw?

Ewen Says: Naw
Twitter Says: Aye 82%; Naw 18%
You Say: **Aye** or **Naw**?

QUESTION 401
21.2.23 – Pancake Day

It is Mardi Gras in New Orleans today – 'Mardi Gras' means Happy Tuesday. Is this true? Aye or Naw?

Ewen Says: Naw
Twitter Says: Aye 27%; Naw 73%
You Say: **Aye** or **Naw**?

QUESTION 402
22.2.23 – Actor Drew Barrymore's forty-eighth birthday

The second highest grossing film Drew Barrymore starred in is *Charlie's Angels*. Is this true? Aye or Naw?

Ewen Says: Naw
Twitter Says: Aye 45%; Naw 55%
You Say: **Aye** or **Naw**?

QUESTION 403
23.2.23 – Toast Day

Eggs are the favourite toast topping in the UK.
Is this true? Aye or Naw?

Ewen Says: Aye
Twitter Says: Aye 33%; Naw 67%
You Say: **Aye** or **Naw**?

QUESTION 404
24.2.23

Starfish don't have brains. Is this true? Aye or Naw?

Ewen Says: Naw
Twitter Says: Aye 38%; Naw 62%
You Say: **Aye** or **Naw**?

QUESTION 405
27.2.23 – Polar Bear Day

There are NO polar bears in Antarctica.
Is this true? Aye or Naw?

Ewen Says: Aye
Twitter Says: Aye 82%; Naw 18%
You Say: **Aye** or **Naw**?

QUESTION 406
28.2.23

The most popular colour of car in the UK in 2023 is grey. Is this true? Aye or Naw?

Ewen Says: Aye
Twitter Says: Aye 45%; Naw 55%
You Say: **Aye** or **Naw**?

QUESTION 407
1.3.23

Sharks sneeze at least once an hour to clear their nostrils. Is this true? Aye or Naw?

Ewen Says: Naw
Twitter Says: Aye 36%; Naw 64%
You Say: **Aye** or **Naw**?

QUESTION 408
2.3.23 – World Book Day

In 2022 more eBooks were sold than actual books. Is this true? Aye or Naw?

Ewen Says: Aye
Twitter Says: Aye 58%; Naw 42%
You Say: **Aye** or **Naw**?

QUESTION 409
3.3.23

Tom Cruise is older than George Clooney.
Is this true? Aye or Naw?

Ewen Says: Naw
Twitter Says: Aye 54%; Naw 46%
You Say: **Aye** or **Naw**?

QUESTION 410
6.3.23 – National Tennis Day

Andy Murray has played in eleven Grand Slam
Finals. Is this true? Aye or Naw?

Ewen Says: Aye
Twitter Says: Aye 63%; Naw 37%
You Say: **Aye** or **Naw**

QUESTION 411
7.3.23 – Alexander Graham Bell Day

Over 60% of children aged ten or under have
mobile phones in the UK. Is this true? Aye or Naw?

Ewen Says: Naw
Twitter Says: Aye 75%; Naw 25%
You Say: **Aye** or **Naw**

QUESTION 412
8.3.23 – International Women's Day

According to *Forbes* magazine, Kamala Harris is the most powerful woman in the world. Is this true? Aye or Naw?

Ewen Says: Naw
Twitter Says: Aye 37%; 63%
You Say: **Aye** or **Naw**

QUESTION 413
9.3.23

The plural of the same kind of fish is fish.
Is this true? Aye or Naw?

Ewen Says: Aye
Twitter Says: Aye 86%; Naw 14%
You Say: **Aye** or **Naw**

QUESTION 414
10.3.23

Venice has more canals than Amsterdam.
Is this true? Aye or Naw?

Ewen Says: Naw
Twitter Says: Aye 46%; Naw 54%
You Say: **Aye** or **Naw**

QUESTION 415
20.3.23 – National Proposal Day

According to Instagram the most popular place in the world to get engaged is Central Park in New York. Is this true? Aye or Naw?

Ewen Says: Aye
Twitter Says: Aye 35%; Naw 65%
You Say: **Aye** or **Naw**

QUESTION 416
21.3.23 – Twitter is seventeen years old today

The most followed person on Twitter on this date is Barack Obama. Is this true? Aye or Naw?

Ewen Says: Aye
Twitter Says: Aye 39%; Naw 61%
You Say: **Aye** or **Naw**

QUESTION 417
22.3.23 – National Seal Day

Seals can only sleep on land. Is this true? Aye or Naw?

Ewen Says: Naw
Twitter Says: Aye 55%; Naw 45%
You Say: **Aye** or **Naw**

QUESTION 418
23.3.23 – National Maths Day

A jiffy is an actual unit of time. Is this true? Aye or Naw?

Ewen Says: Aye
Twitter Says: Aye 38%; Naw 62%
You Say: **Aye** or **Naw**

QUESTION 419
24.3.23 – Day before Scotland v Cyprus, Euro Qualifier

Scotland have won all previous seven international fixtures against Cyprus. Is this true? Aye or Naw?

Ewen Says: Aye
Twitter Says: Aye 58%; Naw 42%
You Say: **Aye** or **Naw**

QUESTION 420
28.3.23 – Scotland v Spain tonight (2–0 win woohoo!!)

Scotland have collectively won and drawn more games against Spain than they have lost. Is this true? Aye or Naw?

Ewen Says: Aye
Twitter Says: Aye 53%; Naw 47%
You Say: **Aye** or **Naw**

QUESTION 421
31.3.23 – Eiffel Tower Day

The Eiffel Tower is 30m (98ft) higher now than when it first opened in 1889. Is this true? Aye or Naw?

Ewen Says: Naw
Twitter Says: Aye 39%; Naw 61%
You Say: **Aye** or **Naw**

You are smashing this! For answers on bubble-wrap, steak-pie, swearing, sausage dogs and starfish **turn to page 256.**

Best Job in the World?

Aye or Naw?

I know I'm very lucky. Anyone who makes a living from talking, playing great music and hanging about with their friends should remember just how lucky we are.

Since my last book there have been so many ridiculous and fun moments. Here are some of the highlights:

Boogie on the Boat

Five hundred party animals on a trip to Amsterdam with Forth 1's fabulous Breakfast crew, Boogie, Arlene and Marty. I managed to sneak on as a stowaway! Every ship needs a Cat.

Absolute madness from the start to finish with blistering DJ sets from the main man himself, Garry Spence and Callum Gallacher. The school disco themed party night on the way home was hilarious. I've never seen so many prosecco drinking Crayola Crayons on a dance floor before. 10/10 team. Great fun.

Matt v Kaye

We had a right laugh backing two of our friends who just happened to be starring in *Strictly Come Dancing*. Ewen chose his bestie Matt Goss and I went with Kaye Adams, who is a lovely lady who lets me borrow her dog. Neither won, but we enjoyed our tango with the glitterball crew.

Jackie Bird v Lewis Capaldi

The celebrity battle you never knew you needed. Lewis thought Jackie was angry with him for saying a naughty word at an Awards Show she hosted. Jackie came on our show, said she was fine with it all and offered to duet with him. She is a cracking singer, so I'd love to make this happen. They could be the new Kenny and Dolly.

Bowie on the Bus

On Cash for Kids Day I ended up doing the 'Clyde Tunnel' challenge dressed as Mr Stay Puff from *Ghostbusters* with the *Bowie at Breakfast* team. This is where you keep singing a song in the tunnel when the radio cuts out, until it comes back on again and hopefully, you'll be at the right bit and in the right key. George, dressed as George Michael, held his tune well; Cassi nailing it as Kylie added the glamour. I was just very sweaty, couldn't see and regretted my outfit choice massively. However, we met a local primary school who made a donation, and they loved big inflatable marshmallowy me, so that made it all worthwhile.

Rewind

We seem to enjoy dressing up and working at this eighties festival at Scone Palace is an absolute hoot. The stars all seem so grateful to still be gigging while the audience are old enough to know better and young enough not to care. Ewen turning into a giggly teen drooling over Claire Grogan was fun to observe. He was dressed as Maverick from *Top Gun*. We met about fifty co-pilots! This year I murdered karaoke with Martin Kemp. Great fun!

What's the Story in *Balamory*

Wouldn't you like to know? We celebrated the 20th anniversary of the children's telly show with Miss Hoolie (Julie Wilson Nimmo) and PC Plum (Andrew Agnew) on the show. They were hilarious sharing behind the scenes chat and PC Plum even let us try on his actual helmet!

Aberdeen Adventure

Greigsy offered to take Producer Cat and I out for dinner in his hometown, the Granite City. We ended up on a pub crawl of the docks and dinner was a £2.40 cheese toasty served in one of the bars. Magic!

Liz Looks for Love

Sometimes on a Monday we will do a little feature called 'three-word weekend' where listeners describe their weekend in just three words. Liz sent in a message saying 'BLIND-DATE AMAZING'. We needed to know more. Over the next few weeks, we spoke to lovely Liz, who was smitten with her new fellow on date one, sort of enjoyed date two, but by date three he was toast. We were worried she had a broken heart, to which she chirpily replied: 'No chance, I'm already messaging someone else!' I hope she finds her Mr Right eventually.

Dublin

Big Boss Victoria, Arlene from Forth 1 Breakfast and I decided to have a quiet reflective weekend in Dublin to see the sights. We were the sights! We met three old men in a bar (sounds like a joke) all over eighty years old, who gave us a list of their favourite pubs to sample. They were full of the craic and reminded me of my dad and his patter so much. We went into that bar for one and left three hours later.

Amy Macdonald

We've been mates with Amy since she first burst onto the scene aged seventeen. Watching her sell out the Hydro and absolutely blow the roof off the place with her sensational set was joyous. What a warm-up to her biggest gig of the year – my fiftieth birthday party two days later. A bonkers night in which the line-up also included PC Plum from *Balamory* singing Rick Astley, Michelle McManus, BGT's Edward Reid, May and Robert Miller, Jane Henderson and a GBX set to finish. I should have sold tickets and made it a festival!

The Edinburgh Fringe

Our live outside broadcast from the Assembly Gardens involved many top acts coming on for a quick interview then heading off to their respective gigs. It was fast, fun and chaotic. My favourite pairing was Irish comedian Jason Byrne with purple puppet Randy Feltface. Ewen and I both had tears laughing at them. We then ended up on a night out with Amy Macdonald with her husband Richard Foster, we met Jason for a drink, and John Bishop turned up to meet him. This had the makings of a belter but Ewen insisted that Amy, Foz and I joined him at a 'cult adult magic show' he'd blagged tickets for. After five minutes I wished they'd made me disappear.

Ewen and Cat Uncut

We started a podcast this year with our friends at G4 Claims for anyone looking for a more adult and unfiltered version of our show and series one has been so much fun to film and record. Our guests have been phenomenal; Greg Hemphill and Julie Nimmo Wilson, The Dolls, Sanjeev Kholi and Mark Cox, Gavin Mitchell, Amy Macdonald, Michelle McManus, Matt Goss, Megara Furie, Paul Riley, Jane McCarry and Karen Dunbar. All massively talented people with incredible stories to share. Will there be a series two? Watch this space ...

Mysterious Girl

Great fun on stage with Peter Andre at the Cash for Kids Christmas lunch raising over £400,000 for the charity. He even opened his shirt and after all those years he still has the abs. He's obviously never had chips and cheese in his life.

So, is it the best job in the world? Apart from being a professional Freddo tester I'm going to say – AYE!!

April – June 2023

QUESTION 422
3.4.23 – Hollywood A-lister Samuel L Jackson was spotted at Bongos Bingo in Glasgow at the weekend. (I was there but missed him as my pal Steph won a Henry Hoover and we were far too excited by that!)

The 'L' in Samuel L Jackson stands for Leon. Is this true? Aye or Naw?

Ewen Says: Naw
Twitter Says: Aye 77%; Naw 23%
You Say: **Aye** or **Naw**?

QUESTION 423
4.4.23 – World Rat Day

Rats giggle if you tickle them. Is this true? Aye or Naw?

Ewen Says: Aye
Twitter Says: Aye 41%; Naw 59%
You Say: **Aye** or **Naw**?

HA HA
HA HA
HA'

QUESTION 424
5.4.23

There are over two thousand road bridges in Scotland.
Is this true? Aye or Naw?

Ewen Says: Naw
Twitter Says: Aye 73%; Naw 27%
You Say: **Aye** or **Naw**?

QUESTION 425
6.4.23 – Tartan Day

Black Watch is the most popular tartan in the world.
Is this true? Aye or Naw?

Ewen Says: Aye
Twitter Says: Aye 52%; Naw 48%
You Say: **Aye** or **Naw**?

QUESTION 426
7.4.23 – US Masters is underway

The highest number of 'hole in ones' in one round
by one player is three. Is this true? Aye or Naw?

Ewen Says: Aye
Twitter Says: Aye 42%; Naw 58%
You Say: **Aye** or **Naw**?

QUESTION 427
10.4.23

Over 16 million Americans think chocolate milk
comes from brown cows. Is this true? Aye or Naw?

Ewen Says: Aye
Twitter Says: Aye 52%; Naw 48%
You Say: **Aye** or **Naw**?

11.4.23 – *River City* stars Stephen Purdon and
Jordan Young join us on the show.

There are more episodes of River City than all seasons
of *Dallas*, *Dynasty* and *Knots Landing* added together.
Is this true? Aye or Naw?

Ewen Says: Naw
Twitter Says: Aye 73%; Naw 27%
You Say: **Aye** or **Naw**?

QUESTION 429
12.4.23

Volkswagen make and sell more sausages than cars.
Is this true? Aye or Naw?

Ewen Says: Aye
Twitter Says: Aye 37%; Naw 63%
You Say: **Aye** or **Naw**?

QUESTION 430
13.4.23 – National Scrabble Day

In a game of Scrabble, the word QUIZ will score
you more than JAZZ. Is this true? Aye or Naw?

Ewen Says: Naw
Twitter Says: Aye 48%; Naw 52%
You Say: **Aye** or **Naw**?

QUESTION 431
14.4.23 – The Grand National takes place this weekend.

In the Grand National, which began in 1839,
only four grey horses have ever won.
Is this true? Aye or Naw?

Ewen Says: Naw
Twitter Says: Aye 72%; Naw 28%
You Say: **Aye** or **Naw**?

QUESTION 432
17.4.23 – Schools go back after the Easter break.
Ewen wants schoolchildren-friendly questions. I know
kids love animals and laughing about poop!

Wombats poop in perfect circular balls.
Is this true? Aye or Naw?

Ewen Says: Aye
Twitter Says: Aye 60%; Naw 40%
You Say: **Aye** or **Naw**?

QUESTION 433
18.4.23 – Today's school subject is science.

Red blood cells are bigger than white blood cells.
Is this true? Aye or Naw?

Ewen Says: Naw
Twitter Says: Aye 49%; Naw 51%
You Say: **Aye** or **Naw**?

QUESTION 434
19.4.23 – School subject today is Geography.

China is the second biggest country in the world.
Is this true? Aye or Naw?

Ewen Says: Naw
Twitter Says: Aye 43%; Naw 57%
You Say: **Aye** or **Naw**?

QUESTION 435
20.4.23 – School subject today is Classical Studies.

In Greek mythology Diana is the goddess of love.
Is this true? Aye or Naw?

Ewen Says:
Twitter Says: Aye 31%; Naw 69%
You Say: **Aye** or **Naw**?

QUESTION 436
21.4.23 – School subject today is History.

The Battle of Bannockburn took place in 1320.
Is this true? Aye or Naw?

Ewen Says: Naw he's convinced it's 1366!
Twitter Says: Aye 13%; Naw 87%
You Say: **Aye** or **Naw**?

QUESTION 437
24.4.23

It rains diamonds on Uranus. Is this true? Aye or Naw?

Ewen Says: Naw
Twitter Says: Aye 38%; Naw 62%
You Say: **Aye** or **Naw**?

QUESTION 438
25.4.23

Frankie Goes to Hollywood's 'Relax' was the biggest
selling single of the 1980s. Is this true? Aye or Naw?

Ewen Says: Aye
Twitter Says: Aye 50%; Naw 50%
You Say: **Aye** or **Naw**?

QUESTION 439
26.4.23 – Alien Day

More people have travelled to space than have reached
the summit of Mount Everest. Is this true? Aye or Naw?

Ewen Says: Naw
Twitter Says: Aye 23%; Naw 77%
You Say: **Aye** or **Naw**?

QUESTION 440
27.4.23

Bad by Michael Jackson was the bestselling album
of the entire 1980s. Is this true? Aye or Naw?

Ewen Says: Aye
Twitter Says: Aye 58%; Naw 42%
You Say: **Aye** or **Naw**?

QUESTION 441
28.4.23

(What's the Story) Morning Glory? by Oasis was the
bestselling album in the entire 1990s.
Is this true? Aye or Naw?

Ewen Says: Naw
Twitter Says: Aye 76%; Naw 24%
You Say: **Aye** or **Naw**?

QUESTION 442
2.5.23

ABBA's *Greatest Hits* was the bestselling album in
the UK in the entire 1970s. Is this true? Aye or Naw?

Ewen Says: Aye
Twitter Says: Aye 47%; Naw 53%
You Say: **Aye** or **Naw**?

QUESTION 443
3.5.23

On the iconic Beatles album *Abbey Road* you can see six
white stripes of the zebra crossing. Is this true? Aye or Naw?

Ewen Says: Aye
Twitter Says: Aye 63%; Naw 37%
You Say: **Aye** or **Naw**?

QUESTION 444
4.5.23 – Star Wars Day. (Again ... yawn!)

The voice of Chewbacca was created using the sound
of four animals: a badger, a lion, a seal and a walrus.
Is this true? Aye or Naw?

Ewen Says: Naw
Twitter Says: Aye 29%; Naw 71%
You Say: **Aye** or **Naw**?

QUESTION 445
9.5.23 – Eurovision build-up week. Ewen's 'specialist subject'.

Sweden have won the Eurovision Song Contest more than any other country. Is this true? Aye or Naw?

Ewen Says: Naw
Twitter Says: Aye 33%; Naw 67%
You Say: **Aye** or **Naw**?

QUESTION 446
10.5.23

There have been five barefoot winners of Eurovision. Is this true? Aye or Naw?

Ewen Says: Aye
Twitter Says: Aye 59%; Naw 41%
You Say: **Aye** or **Naw**?

QUESTION 447
11.5.23

Cyprus have finished last in Eurovision more than any other country. Is this true? Aye or Naw?

Ewen Says: Naw
Twitter Says: Aye 35%; Naw 65%
You Say: **Aye** or **Naw**?

QUESTION 448
12.5.23

UK Eurovision entrant Mae Muller once starred in a
video for Kylie Minogue when she was a little girl.
Is this true? Aye or Naw?

Ewen Says: Aye
Twitter Says: Aye 55%; Naw 45%
You Say: **Aye** or **Naw**?

QUESTION 449
15.5.23 – Sweden win Eurovision 2023

A 'Swedish Kiss' involves a small lick to the
tip of the nose. Is this true? Aye or Naw?

Ewen Says: Naw
Twitter Says: Aye 43%; Naw 57%
You Say: **Aye** or **Naw**?

QUESTION 450
16.5.23

The first engine-powered double decker bus was
invented in Paris. Is this true? Aye or Naw?

Ewen Says: Aye
Twitter Says: Aye 31%; Naw 69%
You Say: **Aye** or **Naw**?

QUESTION 451
17.5.23

There are more bathrooms in the White House than Buckingham Palace. Is this true? Aye or Naw?

Ewen Says: Aye
Twitter Says: Aye 50%; Naw 50%
You Say: **Aye** or **Naw**?

QUESTION 452
18.5.23 – National Numbers Day

If you add the numbers on the side of the famous cars 'Herbie' and 'The General Lee' together, the answer is less than 60. Is this true? Aye or Naw?

Ewen Says: Naw
Twitter Says: Aye 56%; Naw 46%
You Say: **Aye** or **Naw**?

QUESTION 453
19.5.23 – Beyoncé plays Murrayfield this weekend.

Beyoncé's real name is Betty. Is this true? Aye or Naw?

Ewen Says: Aye
Twitter Says: Aye 23%; Naw 77%
You Say: **Aye** or **Naw**?

QUESTION 454
22.5.23

Sherlock Holmes was originally called
'Sherrinford Hope'. Is this true? Aye or Naw?

Ewen Says: Aye
Twitter Says: Aye 22%; Naw 78%
You Say: **Aye** or **Naw**?

QUESTION 455
23.5.23

There were more episodes of US sitcom *Friends*
than *Cheers*. Is this true? Aye or Naw?

Ewen Says: Naw
Twitter Says: Aye 64%; Naw 36%
You Say: **Aye** or **Naw**?

QUESTION 456
24.5.23

There are more than 90,000 seconds in a day.
Is this true? Aye or Naw?

Ewen Says: Naw
Twitter Says: Aye 37%; Naw 63%
You Say: **Aye** or **Naw**?

QUESTION 457
25.5.23 – The morning following the sad passing of
music icon Tina Turner.

There is a Tina Turner Highway. Is this true? Aye or Naw?

Ewen Says: Aye
Twitter Says: Aye 83%; Naw 17%
You Say: **Aye** or **Naw**?

QUESTION 458
26.5.23 – Edinburgh Marathon weekend

The first ever marathon took places in New York.
Is this true? Aye or Naw?

Ewen Says: Aye
Twitter Says: Aye 32%; Naw 68%
You Say: **Aye** or **Naw**?

QUESTION 459
5.6.23

All ladybirds are female. Is this true? Aye or Naw?

Ewen Says: Aye
Twitter Says: Aye 26%; Naw 74%
You Say: **Aye** or **Naw**?

QUESTION 460
6.6.23 – National Eyewear Day – again (The stats are different from last year and the previous related question!)

Over 75% of the population wears glasses or has had corrective eye surgery. Is this true? Aye or Naw?

Ewen Says: Naw
Twitter Says: Aye 55%; Naw 45%
You Say: **Aye** or **Naw**?

QUESTION 461
7.6.23 – National Video Cassette Day

Titanic is the bestselling movie on VHS of all time. Is this true? Aye or Naw?

Ewen Says: Aye
Twitter Says: Aye 38%; Naw 62%
You Say: **Aye** or **Naw**?

QUESTION 462
8.6.23 – World Ocean Day

Sharks have more teeth than slugs. Is this true? Aye or Naw?

Ewen Says: Naw
Twitter Says: Aye 59%; Naw 41%
You Say: **Aye** or **Naw**?

QUESTION 463
9.6.23

The Rolling Stones are the only band in the world to have played on every continent. Is this true? Aye or Naw?

Ewen Says: Naw
Twitter Says: Aye 47%; Naw 53%
You Say: **Aye** or **Naw**?

QUESTION 464
12.6.23 – Superman Day

Superman's middle name is Joseph.
Is this true? Aye or Naw?

Ewen Says: Aye
Twitter Says: Aye 43%; Naw 57%
You Say: **Aye** or **Naw?**

QUESTION 465
13.6.23

There are over 300 flavours of KitKat in Japan.
Is this true? Aye or Naw?

Ewen Says: Aye
Twitter Says: Aye 35%; Naw 65%
You Say: **Aye** or **Naw**?

QUESTION 466

14.6.23 – At eighty-three, Tom Jones starts his eleven country European Tour today.

Sir Tom Jones loves Terry's Chocolate Oranges so much he had them flown over to America when he was on tour. Is this true? Aye or Naw?

Ewen Says: Aye
Twitter Says: Aye 70%; Naw 30%
You Say: **Aye** or **Naw**?

QUESTION 467

15.6.23 – World Tapas Day

'Gambas al ajillo' (garlic prawns) are the most popular tapas dish. Is this true? Aye or Naw?

Ewen Says: Naw
Twitter Says: Aye 41%; Naw 59%
You Say: **Aye** or **Naw**?

QUESTION 468

16.6.23 – Norway play Scotland tomorrow in Oslo for a Euro Qualifier.

There is a village called Aberdeen in Norway. Is this true? Aye or Naw?

Ewen Says: Naw
Twitter Says: Aye 68%; Naw 32%
You Say: **Aye** or **Naw**?

QUESTION 469

19.6.23 – Scotland beat Norway 2–1 with a late winner.

Scotland's winning goal hero Kenny McLean also represented his country at squash. Is this true? Aye or Naw?

Ewen Says: Naw
Twitter Says: Aye 56%; Naw 44%
You Say: **Aye** or **Naw**?

QUESTION 470

20.6.23 – Scotland play Georgia at Hampden in another Euro Qualifier.

The population of Georgia the country is higher than Georgia the U.S. state. Is this true? Aye or Naw?

Ewen Says: Naw
Twitter Says: Aye 29%; Naw 71%
You Say: **Aye** or **Naw**?

QUESTION 471

21.6.23 – Scotland beat Georgia 2–0 in a game delayed for ninety minutes to clear the water-logged pitch.

The longest football match in history lasted over three and a half hours. Is this true? Aye or Naw?

Ewen Says: Aye
Twitter Says: Aye 26%; Naw 74%
You Say: **Aye** or **Naw**?

QUESTION 472

22.6.23 – The Royal Highland Show opens in Ingliston today.

There will be competitors from over fifty countries taking part in the sheep shearing competition at the Royal Highland Show. Is this true? Aye or Naw?

Ewen Says: Aye
Twitter Says: Aye 72%; Naw 38%
You Say: **Aye** or **Naw**?

QUESTION 473

23.6.23 – The Proclaimers play the Big Top in Queens Park, Glasgow, tomorrow.

Charlie is the guitar-playing Proclaimer. Is this true? Aye or Naw?

Ewen Says: Naw
Twitter Says: Aye 26%; Naw 74%
You Say: **Aye** or **Naw**?

QUESTION 474

26.6.23 – Last night Elton John played his final UK gig, headlining Glastonbury.

Elton John's piano is worth more than £2 million. Is this true? Aye or Naw?

Ewen Says: Naw
Twitter Says: Aye 74%; Naw 26%
You Say: **Aye** or **Naw**?

QUESTION 475
27.6.23 – Guns N' Roses play Glasgow tonight.

Guns N' Roses' highest placed single in the UK was
'Knocking on Heaven's Door'. Is this true? Aye or Naw?

Ewen Says: Naw
Twitter Says: Aye 45%; Naw 55%
You Say: **Aye** or **Naw**?

QUESTION 476
28.6.23 – *Wheel of Fortune* announces a return with
Graham Norton as host.

Jenny Powell co-presented more episodes of *Wheel of
Fortune* than Carol Smillie. Is this true? Aye or Naw?

Ewen Says: Aye
Twitter Says: Aye 51%; Naw 49%
You Say: **Aye** or **Naw**?

QUESTION 477
29.6.23 – The name iPhone was registered
twenty years ago today.

The 'I' in iPhone stands for intelligent.
Is this true? Aye or Naw?

Ewen Says: Aye
Twitter Says: Aye 39%; Naw 61%
You Say: **Aye** or **Naw**?

A hedgehog would beat a porcupine in
a 20m sprint. Is this true? Aye or Naw?

Ewen Says: Naw
Twitter Says: Aye 46%; Naw 54%
You Say: **Aye** or **Naw**?

And this, my friends, is where we have to leave the topical questions because of print and publishing deadlines, but dinnae worry, there's a wee bonus section coming your way. Will you get the full promised quota of 500 questions? AYE!!

The answers from this section are on page 260.

Greatest Hits Radio

Fancy a cheeky wee bonus section? Aye . . .

In April 2023 we launched Greatest Hits Radio in Scotland. The stations formerly known as Clyde 2, Forth 2, Tay 2, Westsound, Radio Borders, Northsound 2 and MFR2 are now under one name.

While there are sentimental reasons to hold these brands close to our hearts, our new home has so much potential and we are loving being the first national commercial breakfast show for Scotland.

There are so many big names on the station, let's have some fun and share some secrets.

All of these statements were given to me by the presenters in question. But are they true?

You have to decide . . . AYE or NAW?

Bonus

QUESTION 479

Fred MacAulay can identify any variety of potato
by its leaves. Is this true? Aye or Naw?

You Say: **Aye** or **Naw**?

QUESTION 480

Ken Bruce trained as a lawyer before embarking
on a radio career. Is this true? Aye or Naw?

You Say: **Aye** or **Naw**?

QUESTION 481

Ewen once ran naked around Ibrox after losing a bet about
Rangers signing Dado Prso. Is this true? Aye or Naw?

You Say: **Aye** or **Naw**?

QUESTION 482

Jackie Brambles appeared in the film *Four Weddings and a Funeral*. Is this true? Aye or Naw?

You Say: **Aye** or **Naw**?

QUESTION 483

Webster once won a competition for having the best snake. Is this true? Aye or Naw?

You Say: **Aye** or **Naw**?

QUESTION 484

Boogie once asked Baby Spice out on a date. Is this true? Aye or Naw?

You Say: **Aye** or **Naw**?

QUESTION 485

Arlene had her head shaved as a kid after an incident with her brother and blunt scissors. Is this true? Aye or Naw?

You Say: **Aye** or **Naw**?

QUESTION 486

Andy Crane once locked himself in a hotel toilet and had
to be rescued by reception staff. Is this true? Aye or Naw?

You Say: **Aye** or **Naw**?

QUESTION 487

Fred MacAulay has flown a Tornado jet around Scotland.
Is this true? Aye or Naw?

You Say: **Aye** or **Naw**?

QUESTION 488

Ken Bruce owns and drives a bus. Is this true? Aye or Naw?

You Say: **Aye** or **Naw**?

QUESTION 489

Ewen once tried to chat up TV presenter
Clare Balding at the races while jockey Willie Carson
looked on. Is this true? Aye or Naw?

You Say: **Aye** or **Naw**?

QUESTION 490

Jackie Brambles applied to join the CIA.
Is this true? Aye or Naw?

You Say: **Aye** or **Naw**?

QUESTION 491

Webster won a piggyback race on the back of the
World's Strongest Man. Is this true? Aye or Naw?

You Say: **Aye** or **Naw**?

QUESTION 492

Boogie sang 'Highway to Hell' with a live band
at his wedding. Is this true? Aye or Naw?

You Say: **Aye** or **Naw**?

QUESTION 493

Arlene won a school spelling competition by being able
to correctly spell diarrhoea. Is this true? Aye or Naw?

You Say: **Aye** or **Naw**?

QUESTION 494

Andy Crane has starred in *Eastenders*?
Is this true? Aye or Naw?

You Say: **Aye** or **Naw**?

QUESTION 495

Fred MacAulay swam across the River Tay
for charity. Is this true? Aye or Naw?

You Say: **Aye** or **Naw**?

QUESTION 496

Ken Bruce plays in a band called No Direction.
Is this true? Aye or Naw?

You Say: **Aye** or **Naw**?

QUESTION 497

Ewen once modelled swimwear for a department
store in Dubai. Is this true? Aye or Naw?

You Say: **Aye** or **Naw**?

QUESTION 498

Jackie Brambles is related to Britney Spears.
Is this true? Aye or Naw?

You Say: **Aye** or **Naw**?

QUESTION 499

Webster's nipples are too small to pierce.
Is this true? Aye or Naw?

You Say: **Aye** or **Naw**?

QUESTION 500

Arlene dipped her boob in tomato soup when she first
met her potential in-laws. Is this true? Aye or Naw?

You Say: **Aye** or **Naw**?

And with that lovely vision … We have reached our magic number of 500 questions.

The answers from this section are on page 265.

Answers

JAN – MARCH 21

1. NAW – The Sultan of Brunei has never spent £20,000 on Irn-Bru for a Burns Supper.
2. AYE – The shortest street in the world according to the *Guinness Book of Records* is Ebeneezer Place in Wick, a teeny 6ft 9in long.
3. NAW – Gerry Butler trained as a lawyer before becoming an actor.
4. NAW – Queen Victoria was famously anti-smoking. However, she did have staff to smoke out the midges on her behalf! Perks of being royalty!
5. NAW – This was made up by Producer Carnage. No Scottish or Finnish Grannies were harmed in the process.
6. AYE – New Order's hit 'Blue Monday' was in the Independent Singles Chart for 185 weeks.
7. AYE – Scotland have qualified for NINE World Cups, but only played in eight! We declined our place in 1950. Google for the full story but we held our moral high ground. It is a long and fascinating tale involving FIFA, the war and sporting integrity.
8. AYE – Brigadier Sir Nils Olav the Third has the rank of Colonel in Chief of the Norwegian Kings Guard.

9. AYE – John Henry Anderson, 'The Wizard of the North', who was born in 1814 in Aberdeenshire, is widely regarded as the man who popularised this trick. Some historians claim it was first seen in Paris a hundred years before, but we are claiming it!

10. AYE – Bill Murray did indeed gatecrash a student party in St Andrews, where he famously had some vodka, sang with a guitar player, did the dishes and then left.

11. AYE – Jackson was a massive fan of Burns. His pal David Guest once revealed: '"Thriller" was inspired by "Tam O' Shanter".' Together they put some of Burns poems to contemporary music.

12. AYE – Peter Dodds McCormick was an Australian school-teacher who was originally born in Port Glasgow, Scotland. He wrote the Australian National anthem.

13. AYE – Chicken Tikka Masala was invented in the Shish Mahal restaurant in Glasgow by chef Ali Ahmed Aslam, who added a tin of condensed tomato soup and some yoghurt to a curry to placate a customer who didn't like his food too spicy! The rest is history.

14. NAW – The River Tay is the longest river in Scotland. 1) Tay – 188km, 2) Spey 172km, 3) Clyde 170km.

15. NAW – Edinburgh had the first fire brigade in the world. The Edinburgh Fire Engine Establishment was started in 1824 by James Braidwood. London was next, eight years later in 1832.

16. AYE – Dull, Boring and Bland are all twinned. I bet they are anything but . . .

17. NAW – The origins of ice skating lie in Scandinavia, and most likely Finland, where locals used whale and elk bone to move across the ice. The first speed skating event was held in Norway, while the first figure skating event was held in Vienna.

18. AYE – According to a Government website, Scotland has 63% of the coastline of the UK. Scotland has 18,672km/

11,602 miles to be precise, which includes islands. England has 4428km/2748 miles, so Scotland is over three times longer.

19. AYE – Believe it or not there is an old law which can fine kilties two cans of beer for wearing pants! It was written in 1935 and is thought to have been the result of a legal joke, but it still stands. So, pay up, boys!

20. NAW – Loch Lomond does not hold more fresh water than all the lochs and lakes in England and Wales combined; however, Loch Ness does!!!

21. NAW – Pac-Man was invented in Japan in 1980.

22. AYE – Some of the remains of St Valentine rest in the Church of Blessed John Duns Scotus in the Gorbals in Glasgow. It's thought the casket contains remains of his forearm bone and was brought to the city by Franciscan Monks in 1863.

23. AYE – There are thirty-three registered places called Aberdeen in the world, including Hong Kong, Canada, Australia and South Africa.

24. NAW – Berti Vogts probably fielded a few donkeys in his time, but he never owned a Llama.

25. AYE – Clapshot is neeps and tatties mashed together sometimes with butter, cream and seasoning.

26. NAW – Lulu was born in Lennoxtown before moving to Dennistoun.

27. NAW – The name Kirkcaldy comes from the Brythonic words 'caer-caled-din'. Caer = fort, caled = hard, din = hill. Together it means 'fort on the hard hill'. Now you know. ☺

28. AYE – Charles Macintosh, a chemist from Glasgow, invented a waterproof fabric in 1823. He patented this and his raincoat, which became famous as simply a 'Mac'.

29. NAW – The McDonald brothers who invented the fast food chain were the children of Irish immigrants who moved to California.

30. AYE – A tattie-bogle is a Scottish scarecrow: 'tattie' came from the potato sack used for his head, and 'bogle' refers to a spiritual being from folk tales.

31. NAW – As far as I can see there has never been a haggis flavoured jellybean. I think the world is probably OK for this.

32. NAW – The last pterodactyl is thought to have taken to the skies 66 million years ago. Edinburgh Zoo is old, but it's not that old!

33. AYE – The oldest Post Office in the world was opened in Sanquhar High Street in 1712.

34. NAW – 'Wellies' or Wellington boots were first invented in 1815 in London. Arthur Wellesley, then Viscount Wellington, asked his shoemaker, Mr George Hoby to design a boot which was easier to wear with his new style of trousers.

35. AYE – The world's oldest football is thought to date back to 1540 and was found behind an oak panel in the Queen's Chambers in Stirling Castle. Mary, Queen of Scotland wrote about her love of playing with the football. It was an inflated pig's bladder wrapped in cowhide and about half the size of footballs used today.

36. AYE – Author Ian Rankin was born in Cardenden, Fife.

37. NAW – Miss Jean Brodie was a character invented by Muriel Spark; however, she was loosely based on Christina Kay, a teacher at Muriel's school.

38. AYE – My granny flew over Rothesay in a WW1 plane, which was the star attraction at a summer fair held at Ettrick Bay and offered rides to brave locals.

39. AYE – There are more sheep than people in Scotland. Sheep – 6.73 million, people – 5.4 million.

40. NAW – There are more cows than pigs in Scotland. Cows – 1.76 million, pigs – 317,000.

41. NAW – There are more Highland cows than goats in Scotland. Highland cows – 15,000, goats – 5,591.

42. AYE – Irn-Bru does contain iron. Each bottle has trace amounts of 0.002 per cent iron in the form of ammonium ferric citrate. That's what happens when you use girders!

43. AYE – Caesar's Palace in Aberdeen was a famous nightclub.

44. AYE – In the 1960s Islay Dunlop Cheese was banned in Italy as it was apparently making people too randy. In fact when the creamery reopened on the island in the nineties there was an unprecedented baby boom!

45. AYE AND NAW! – Experts agree he was born in AD 387 in Old Kilpatrick, Dumbarton (Scotland). However, at the time it was Britannia and under Roman rule. So technically both answers are correct.

46. NAW – Scotland has 790 islands, though only ninety-three of them are inhabited.

47. NAW – No Scottish heroes were ever harmed by dangerous dumpling incidents as far as I am aware.

48. AYE – Brora, a small industrial village, was once known as 'Electric City'. It had thriving industries; coal pits, salt pans, boat building, fish-curing, a woollen mill, brick factory and stone quarry. Brora made headlines when three streetlights were turned on in 1912, before power became available to locals.

49. NAW – Marti Pellow was never a plumber. Wet Wet Wet, oh come on, it's almost amusing.

50. NAW – As much as the Tartan Army would love this to be true, Scotland manager Stevie Clark does not have this tattoo.

APRIL – JUNE 21

51. NAW – Ewen was a nightclub DJ in Dubai but was thankfully never paid to dance erotically.

52. AYE – The Scotch egg originated in London. Fortnum and Mason, the famous London department store, claims to

have created them in 1738 for wealthy travellers going on carriage rides.

53. NAW – On this date, there were 1,197 episodes of *River City* compared to 1,517 of *Take the High Road* (which became *High Road*).

54. AYE – *Supergran* was surprisingly successful abroad after being dubbed into Spanish in the early 2000s.

55. NAW – *Hockey Night* in Canada is the longest running sports show: it has been on the go since 1952.

56. AYE – *Taggart* creator Glen Chandler had a full backstory for his lead character. He was the son of a tram driver from Springburn who would occasionally pinch records from Woolworths to order, including Jimmy Shand records.

57. AYE – Most of the fight scene horses in *Braveheart* were fake. They were 200lb models propelled by nitrogen cylinders and could move at 30mph. After release, there was an investigation by animal welfare officers, who were convinced the horses were real.

58. NAW – There were no fake black pudding otters in *Ring of Bright Water*.

59. NAW – Blair Drummond Safari Park was opened in 1970 by circus leader Jimmy Chipperfield.

60. AYE – In 1838, the 78th Highlanders returned to the castle from a posting in Sri Lanka with an elephant. He stayed in the castle and loved beer, often popping his trunk through the canteen window for a taste of ale. Randomly, his toes are now displayed in the National War Museum in the castle. His name is not recorded.

61. NAW – Annie Lennox is probably just as skilled at navigation as she is at singing.

62. NAW – There are no baby crocodiles at Moat Brae. They'd make any visit too snappy.

63. AYE – Tricky one, as Aye means it isn't and Naw means it is! Dunnet Head is the most Northerly point of mainland Scotland.

64. AYE – Rowing machines are the most popular machine in a gym. 1) Rowing machine, 2) treadmill, 3) stair climber. Ewen had a strop at this answer and phoned a Bannatyne's gym looking for multi-millionaire owner Duncan. He wasn't there, so Stuart, a random PT, answered the call. He said treadmill. Personally, I would agree with that but don't mess with new surveys found on Google!

65. NAW – Scotland has roughly 3,000 castles, Germany has 25,000.

66. NAW – In Scotland it is not illegal to be drunk in charge of a donkey even if it is not to be encouraged! It is, however, an offence to be drunk in charge of a cow or a horse. I loved the fact TV presenter Gail Porter was first to answer this on Twitter saying: 'No it's a cow!' complete with emoji. Udderly brilliant!

67. AYE – Only lady midges have teeth. They need blood for their eggs to grow. Male midges are quite happy sooking on plant nectar and will never bother humans.

68. NAW – My dad did once wake up on a PTFC manager's floor with a Cup, but it was the League Cup, not the Scottish Cup, back in 1971.

69. AYE – There is no such thing as pear cider: it is called perry.

70. AYE – Humans are the only animals that can blush. Some birds can blush, though.

71. AYE – Candy floss was invented in 1897 in Tennessee by William Morrison, who was a dentist. Great way to drum up trade, I suppose!

72. NAW – Hawaii is the best place in the world to see rainbows because the air is exceptionally clean and free of pollution, dust and pollen.

73. AYE – Dr Fredric K. Baur, a chemist by trade, invented the tube in 1966 and was buried in one of his creations in 2008 with the blessing of his family.

74. AYE – Bees have been found at the summit of Everest and scientists have proven in a flight chamber they can fly up to 9000m (29,525ft). Everest is 8849m (29,030ft).

75. AYE – Over eighty-five per cent of toilet paper in France is pink. White is the second favourite option!

76. AYE – In Latin 'Canarie Insulai' means 'Island of Dogs'. When the Romans rediscovered the islands, they were overrun with dogs, hence the name.

77. NAW – Rottweilers have never pulled canal boats; they were, however, once used to heard cattle.

78. AYE – A monkey in a mask was the original plan for Yoda; they even tried one on set and there are historical photos of this, but the monkey proved difficult to direct. Who would have imagined that! Too much monkey business by far!

79. AYE – Everyone can make the 'asparagus pee' smell, but only those with the right olfactory genes can smell it.

80. NAW – A plumber? TAP dancing . . . come on, guys! ☺

81. NAW – Stevie Nicks has no connection to a cycling shop. Although I was inspired to write this question because of their top hit 'The Chain'. Sorry, but that's how my heid works.

82. AYE – At 695,662km², Texas is bigger than any European country.

83. NAW – A langoustine is a member of the lobster family.

84. NAW – Caterpillars have twelve eyes, six on each side.

85. AYE – Donald Duck has a middle name. His full name is Donald Fauntleroy Duck.

86. AYE – Over 4 million Japanese golfers pay the equivalent of £65 a year for £3,500 indemnity against bagging a hole in one. In Japan you must put on a party for friends and family if this happens.

87. NAW – More people live in Turkey than Italy. Turkey – 84.7 million, Italy – 59.1 million.

88. NAW – Chess was invented in India.

89. AYE – French is spoken more widely than Portuguese. French – 300 million, Portuguese – 200 million.

90. AYE – Turkeys have more bones than whales. Turkeys have 200 bones, whales 161.

91. NAW – The Swiss eat the most chocolate in Europe. 1) Switzerland – 19.8lb a year, 2) Germany – 17.4lb, 3) Ireland – 16.3lb, 4) UK – 16.3lb. For comparison, Belgians eat 13.23lb per year.

92. AYE – Finland is the happiest country in the world. It has retained this title since 2018. 1) Finland, 2) Denmark, 3) Switzerland, 4) Iceland, 5) Netherlands.

93. NAW – Skerryvore means 'big rock' and is also a remote island off the west coast of Scotland.

94. AYE – Poland is home to the European bison. They live in the Białowieża Forest, weigh 610kg, are 3m long and can live up to twenty-four years.

95. AYE – Danish pastries are NOT from Denmark. They were invented in 1850 in Vienna, Austria.

96. AYE – The free wine fountain is in the town of Abruzzo on the eastern shoreline of the Adriatic Sea. It has a push button and works like a water fountain.

97. AYE – Spain produces almost half of all olive oil. However, Greeks consume more. Top olive oil producers: 1) Spain, 2) Italy, 3) Tunisia, 4) Greece, 5) Turkey.

98. NAW – People in the Czech Republic consume the most beer in Europe. 1) Czech Rep – 188.6 litres per person per year, 2) Austria – 107.8 litres, 3) Romania – 100.3 litres, 4) Germany – 99 litres, 5) Poland – 97.7 litres.

99. NAW – Food historians say it was either a Russian chef who invented Chicken Kiev for other Europeans or a Parisian chef, both in the 1800s. All agree it did not come from Kiev.

JULY – SEP 21

100. NAW – Austria owns more of the Alps than any other country. Austria owns 28.7%, Italy 27.2%, France 21.4%, Switzerland 13.2%.

101. AYE – Tiramisu is full of ingredients to 'pick you up'.

102. NAW – The furthest a donkey's bray can be heard in a desert is 60 miles.

103. NAW – Italians eat more than three times more pasta per year than Americans. The average Italian will eat 51lb of pasta a year, the average American will eat 15.5lb of pasta.

104. NAW – Whigfield's 'Saturday Night' was always 'Saturday Night'.

105. NAW – Gareth Southgate was never a high-jump champion. He did, however, represent his country at triple jump and was excellent at the 200m.

106. NAW – Status Quo have sold more records than Pavarotti. Status Quo – 120 million, Pavarotti – 100 million.

107. AYE – The world gymnasium comes from the Greek root 'gymnos' meaning naked. The literal translation of gymnasium is naked exercise! The fifteenth Olympics, held in 720BC, are the first with records of naked participation. Hope they got the relay handover correct!

108. AYE – The medals are made from recycled phones. Over 6 million phones were collected in a project involving every city in Japan.

109. NAW – Sadly the Olympics are yet to embrace a pogo-stick race. Boing, boing, boing!

110. NAW – Pankration WAS one of the original sports, but it is basically a fight until the end. It only stopped through submission or death. You were allowed to do everything apart from bite, gouge eyes or squeeze your opponent's delicate bits!

111. AYE – Underwater swimming was a sport in the 1900 Paris Olympics, the only games it was included in. Won by Charles Devendeville, you scored one point for each second under water and two points for each metre swum in a straight line. He swam 60m in 1 minute 8.4 seconds.

112. NAW – Fortune cookies either come from L.A, San Francisco or Japan! The San Francisco bakery Benkyodo and the LA-based Hong Kong Noodle Company both

claim to have invented them in the early 1900s; however, a wood block image from Japan in 1878 shows a street vendor selling them. Either way, they were not invented in China.

113.   AYE – Poles were used to cross canals in the Friesland province in the Netherlands. The first competitions measured distance, not height.

114.   AYE – The beds in the Tokyo Olympics are made from strong recycled cardboard capable of holding 200kg or 31.4 stone.

115.   NAW – Only one athlete has ever won gold at both the summer and winter Olympics. America Eddie Eagan won a boxing gold in Antwerp in 1920 and team bobsleigh gold in 1932 in Lake Placid.

116.   AYE – Sir Chris Hoy loved the film *E.T.* and wanted a BMX after watching it. His first bike cost £5 and between the ages of seven and fourteen he represented Scotland as a BMX rider.

117.   NAW – Worms do not have ears! They don't have eyes either but can sense vibrations in the soil. They do have a mouth but no teeth.

118.   AYE – The Basenji hunting dog from Central Africa can't bark because of its unusually shaped larynx but it can yodel. They are nicknamed 'the barkless dog'.

119.   NAW – The most common phobia in the world is arachnophobia, the fear of spiders. 1) Spiders, 2) snakes, 3) heights, 4) crowds or open spaces, 5) dogs.

120.   AYE – Pule donkey cheese from Serbia costs £600 per lb. Only one farm in the world makes it. It is described as crumbly and soft, with a richer taste than Spanish Manchego.

121.   NAW – As cool as it sounds, there are no flying cats in Brazil.

122.   NAW – The highest rollercoaster in Europe is the Red Force at Ferrari Land in Port Aventura in Spain. It is 120m high, while the Big One is 72m high.

123. AYE – A Tom and Jerry cocktail is a traditional Christmas cocktail in the US made with eggnog, nutmeg, rum, brandy and warm milk. Originally Tom and Jerry were called Jasper and Jinx and got renamed in a competition.

124. AYE – Scientists at Oxford claim goldfish can recognise their owners out of forty-four strangers and can also have memories that last six months.

125. AYE – James Bond was an American ornithologist. Sir Ian Fleming, who wrote the Bond series, admitted in an interview he pinched the name as he loved his books. The two met at the premier of *Goldeneye*. James Bond told Fleming: 'I don't read your books'. Fleming replied, 'I don't blame you.'

126. AYE – Termites fart more than any other living creature and are responsible for 20 million tonnes of methane a year. Do NOT give them sprouts!

127. AYE – It is impossible to hum whilst holding your nose. I hope you tried anyway. ☺

128. AYE – The old Roman calendar started in March, so September was the seventh month. January and February only got added around 700BC.

129. NAW – The average person uses the toilet 2,500 times a year. Although I am not so sure, we all know what happens if you 'break the seal' too early on a night out!

130. AYE – Jarvis Cocker worked in a fishmonger shop, where his main job was scrubbing the crabs.

131. AYE – New research suggests 60–80% of people can roll their tongues.

132. NAW – David Bowie was never a gravedigger – but Rod Stewart was! He worked in the Highgrove Cemetery in London marking out and digging the plots.

133. AYE – The first wedding cakes historically recorded were from Ancient Rome and were made of wheat or barley. They were broken over the bride's head for good luck. Crumbs!

134. AYE – Elephants' tusks are made of dentine; they are basically continuously growing front canine teeth.

135. NAW – The most common date for births in the UK is 26 September. Lots of wee Hogmanay babies. Happy New Year indeed!

136. AYE – The funny bone is NOT a bone; it is a nerve.

137. NAW – North Korea have more submarines than any other country. They have 83, China is second with 74, the US have 66, Russia own 62 and the UK operate 10.

138. AYE – The Portuguese drink the most hot chocolate, averaging 100.2 cups a year. Second is Finland with 90 cups and third is Columbia with 84 cups.

139. AYE – The M6 is made from books: 2.5 million copies of Mills and Boon books were acquired and pulped at a recycling firm and then added to asphalt and tarmac and used in the top layer of the motorway.

140. NAW – Michael Bolton's first professional gig was in a heavy metal band called Blackjack. He did go on to release a classical album, but he started in rock.

OCT – DEC 21

141. NAW – People in India read the most. They read for 10.4 hours a week, averaging 1 hour 15 mins every day. 1) India, 2) Thailand (9.2 hours per week), 3) China (8 hours a week). The UK was placed at No 26 – reading for 5.18 hours per week.

142. NAW – *The Beano* annuals were released before *Oor Wullie*. *Beano* – 1938, *Oor Wullie* – 1940. However, *The Broons* annual was out before them all in 1936. *The Dandy* was also 1938.

143. NAW – Mr Tickle was the first book in the Mr Men series, created after Roger Hargreaves son asked his dad, 'What does a tickle look like?' *Mr Happy* was the third book, after *Mr Tickle* and *Mr Greedy*.

144. NAW – There are more *Famous Five* books than *Secret Seven* books. *Famous Five* – 28, *Secret Seven* – 23.

145. NAW – There was never a 'Barry Potter'.

146. NAW – There are 731,545 people in Alaska and only 30,000 bears. Twenty-four people per bear!

147. NAW – Take That had more No. 1's than the Spice Girls. Spice Girls had nine, Take That have eleven.

148. NAW – The turtle's shell is its skeleton with over fifty bones, including its spine and rib cage.

149. NAW – Kim Kardashian went swimming with dolphins on holiday in Mexico, but she never trained them.

150. AYE – 4.6 million will dress as witches. 1) Witch, 2) rabbit, 3) dinosaur, 4) Spider-Man, 5) Cruella De Vil.

151. AYE – The Count from *Sesame Street* is 1,832,652 years old. That's a lot of cake! Ahh–Ahh!

152. AYE – Chucky creator Don Mancini wondered what would happen if a cute cabbage patch doll turned bad.

153. AYE – The heaviest pumpkin grown this year was a 2,703lb beauty in Italy. Two average Aberdeen Angus cows added together would weigh 2,420lb. No, I have no idea how my brain works either. ☺

154. NAW – COP stands for Conference of the Parties.

155. AYE – Joe Biden once spent $10,000 on Jeni's Splendid Ice Cream for campaign staff and party donors. He famously said: 'I'm Joe Biden – I don't drink, I don't smoke but I do eat a lot of ice cream.'

156. NAW – SWAT stands for Special Weapons and Tactics.

157. AYE – The Pacific Ocean is the largest and the deepest (13,215ft deep, while the Atlantic is 12,880ft deep).

158. AYE – Greta's mum Malena Ernman represented Sweden at Eurovision. She sang 'La Voix' in Moscow in 2009.

159. NAW – Barack Obama has two Spoken Word Grammys. One for *Dreams of My Father* and the other for *The Audacity of Hope*. His wife Michelle has one for *Becoming*.

160. NAW – Alaska is one of the few US states to have more men than women: 110 men per 100 women.

161. NAW – Germany has 48 million registered cars; the UK has 39.2 million.

162. AYE – It takes one-third more energy to make coffee from a machine. £68 million a year is wasted in the UK over-filling and boiling kettles.

163. AYE – In Moldova they use a polenta-like porridge called mamaliga as a side dish, which can be garnished with cottage cheese, sour cream or pork.

164. AYE – Both are considered the oldest, although nobody can quite agree on an exact date. The Danish red flag with white cross was first seen in 1219; the Saltire around the same time but it was previously red not blue. The Danish flag was officially recognised in 1625, while the blue saltire was recognised in the sixteenth century. All a bit confusing but aye, they are ancient!

165. AYE – John Souttar's brother Harry plays for Australia

166. NAW – The average number of friends on Facebook is 338.

167. NAW – Mickey Mouse was originally meant to be called Mortimer Mouse.

168. AYE – The longest game of Monopoly lasted over 70 days– 1,680 hours to be precise. Over 250 million Monopoly games have been sold in 147 countries since 1935 and it is still played by over 1 billion people.

169. NAW – Mr Blobby was meant to represent a chaotic giant pink blancmange, not a mouldy sausage!

170. NAW – The world record for individual sprout eating in one minute is thirty-three.

171. NAW – 154 million crackers are pulled or sold in the UK annually.

172. AYE – Reindeer are the only species of deer to have hairy noses, it is to make the cold air warmer when it hits their lungs. They also have wee hairy hooves.

173. AYE – White Christmas has sold over 50 million copies and had been released over 500 times in many countries.

174. AYE – 'Jingle Bells' was the first song ever played in space during Nasa's Gemini 6A space flight. They connected with Gemini 7 and played the song over the airwaves.

175. NAW – A reindeer can outrun a donkey. Reindeer can run 50km per hour; donkeys' top speed is 24km per hour. There is a reason Santa picked Rudolph and chums!

176. NAW – The average snowman is 5ft 3in. In the UK they are made up of two balls; in the US they prefer three.

177. NAW – Cabbage Patch Kids are the bestselling Christmas toy of all time. 1) Cabbage Patch Kids, 2) Rubik's Cube, 3) Monopoly, 4) Teenage Ninja Turtles, 5) Buzz Lightyear.

178. AYE – The Rockefeller tree is higher than the Murrayfield goalposts. The tree is 79ft high, the posts are 52.5ft high.

179. NAW – *The Grinch* is the highest grossing Christmas film. 1) *The Grinch* – $512m, 2) *Home Alone* – $476m, 3) *How the Grinch Stole Christmas* – $363, 4) *Home Alone 2* – $353, 5) *A Christmas Carol* – $325m.

180. NAW – The average 6ft Christmas tree will have 50 baubles. A perfect decoration chart states the tree size to bauble ratio should be: 3ft/20 baubles, 5ft/40 baubles, 6ft/50 baubles, 7ft/75 baubles.

181. NAW – It was the Ancient Greeks who first kissed under mistletoe. The plant was also used in marriage ceremonies and associated with fertility.

182. NAW – Reindeer droppings have never been an aphrodisiac, ya wee mingers.

JAN – MARCH 22

183. AYE – The Cookie Monster's real name is Sid.

184. NAW – English players have won more World Championships. 14–11 to England. For Scotland Stephen Hendry won six, John Higgins won four and Graeme Dott won once.

185. AYE – The UK grows over 500 varieties of tattie, although only eighty types are grown commercially.

186. AYE – Snoopy was originally called Sniffy. Charles Shultz discovered another Sniffy in a rival cartoon just two days before his strip was printed for the first time.

187. AYE – Sloths do not fart. They avoid gas through the quirk of slow digestion, any gas is simply reabsorbed through their intestine back into their blood stream.

188. NAW – Greyfriars's Bobby was a Skye terrier. However, here is the conspiracy theory – some people believe the original Bobby WAS a mongrel, but the curator of the graveyard invented the story of him never leaving his master's grave to charm tourists and get free lunches at a local restaurant. So, on this occasion, you can be strict or choose to accept both answers.

189. NAW – Jason Donovan never had a successful tennis playing uncle.

190. AYE – Pigs are more intelligent that dogs. They show emotion and empathy, have a great sense of object location memory, they use over twenty sounds to communicate and can play video games better than chimps!

191. NAW – Mount Rushmore is higher than Ben Nevis. Mount Rushmore is 1,754m while Ben Nevis is 1,345m.

192. NAW – Americans eat more cheese per person than any other country. Americans eat 37kg per person per year, French people eat 25kg per person.

193. NAW – Tynecastle was opened before Hampden Park: Tynecastle in 1886, Hampden in 1903.

194. NAW – 52% of the UK prefers crunchy peanut butter.

195. AYE – Rabbie had twelve children to four different mothers, Boris has, well ... We are not really sure, but the conservative (pun intended) guess is seven or eight.

196. AYE – Canberra can be derived from a word meaning cleavage but also from a word meaning meeting place. So, take your pick.

197. AYE – Australia has the largest herd of wild camels in the world with over 1 million feral camels, a population which doubles every nine years.

198. AYE – There are two kazoo museums in the world. One is in Beaufort, South Carolina, the other is in Eden, New York.

199. AYE – Sprouts are an aphrodisiac; they are full of folate, which is good for men's bits!

200. AYE – Chinese New Year follows the lunar calendar so can land on different dates.

201. AYE – Hedgehogs can swim. They can also climb trees!

202. NAW – Annie Lennox worked as a waitress (not in a cocktail bar) but in Pippins Restaurant in Hampstead.

203. AYE – Budgies do not pee. All waste squirts from its bottom. Enjoy your dinner ... ☺

204. NAW – The average car battery in the UK is designed to last three to five years.

205. NAW – There are more days in the year than active cruise ships: currently there are 314 active cruise ships.

206. AYE – The average male shoe size in the UK is size 10. Forty years ago, it was size 8.

207. AYE – The first waterproof umbrella was invented in China over 1,000 years ago when they waxed and lacquered paper brollies. The first umbrella for shade is thought to have been invented in Egypt 4,000 years ago.

208. AYE – *Rolling Stone* magazine voted Jimmy Hendrix as the best guitarist of all time. 1) Jimmy Hendrix, 2) Eric Clapton, 3) Jimmy Page, 4) Keith Richards, 5) Jeff Beck.

209. AYE – An ant can lift over twenty times its body weight. It's the equivalent of a six-year-old child lifting a family car.

210. NAW – My Aunty Jean lives in Helensburgh. She enjoys a trip to Rothesay though for a Zavaroni's cone.

211. AYE – Ewen's Aunty Donna bathed him with a dinosaur sponge. He was thirty-one at the time.

212. NAW – Ants do not have lungs. They have little holes on their body called spiracles, which have air tubes called trachea branching through their entire body.

213. NAW – The Italian Tooth Fairy has a helper, but it is a little mouse called topolino dei denti.

214. AYE – Lemon and sugar remains the UK's favourite pancake topping. 1) Lemon and sugar, 2) sugar, 3) maple syrup, 4) chocolate spread, 5) syrup.

215. NAW – More people live in Livingston than Stirling. Stirling – 36,000, Livingston 57,030.

216. NAW – The average coconut tree produces thirty coconuts a year with up to seventy in optimum conditions.

217. NAW – The dung beetle is the strongest. It can lift 1,141 times its body weight. That is the equivalent of the average person pulling six double decker buses full of passengers.

218. AYE – 78% of households in Scotland still own a landline.

219. NAW – There are more men than women in the world: 101.6 males per 100 females, meaning 49.58% of the population are women.

220. NAW – Barbie was out before Sindy. Barbie was 1959, Sindy was 1963, although Lilly from Germany was out in 1956.

221. NAW – The most popular bagpipe tune is 'Scotland the Brave'.

222. AYE – James is the most popular middle name for a boy in Scotland. 1) James, 2) John, 3) William.

223. AYE – The first three digits of pi are 3.14.

224. NAW – Caesar was fifty-five when he was stabbed to death by sixty conspirators.

225. NAW – Pandas sleep for ten hours max, they spend the other fourteen hours eating. I relate to pandas!

226. NAW – Guinness was first brewed in Dublin in 1759, 126 years before Tennent's began production.

227. AYE – 74% of us are side-sleepers, 16% sleep on their stomach and 10% on their back.

228. AYE – Cats have eighteen toes. Five on each front paw, and four on each back paw.
229. NAW – A grand piano and an upright piano both have eighty-eight keys.
230. NAW – Pop-a-point pencils were invented in Taiwan in the early 1970s.
231. NAW – The average child will go through 750 crayons. First made with charcoal and oil, they are now made of wax. Crayola Crayons first came out in 1903 with eight colours: red, orange, yellow, green, blue, violet, brown and black.

APRIL – JUNE 22

232. NAW – Poopis hillaria?? Come on, guys . . . ☺
233. AYE – Purple carrots are rich in antioxidants, which reduce inflammation and help heart health.
234. AYE – Tunnock's make and sell over 6 million caramel wafers a week using 1.3 metric tonnes of caramel an hour.
235. AYE – The Registrar of Tartans says: 'The Burberry Black has become such a part of the brand it can now be deemed a corporate tartan.'
236. AYE – Edinburgh Zoo was the first in the world to breed penguins, welcoming their first chick in 1919.
237. NAW – The average person eats 2lb of garlic a year.
238. AYE – Students love banana milkshake, voting it No. 1; however, it only comes fourth in the list for everyone else. 1) strawberry, 2) vanilla, 3) chocolate, 4) banana.
239. AYE – Tetley tea is the No. 1 brand in Scotland. In England it is Yorkshire Tea, while in Northern Ireland it is P.G Tips.

240. AYE – Pigs can NOT see the sky. The anatomy of their neck muscles and spine limits the movement of their head and restricts looking upwards.

241. NAW – Elon Musk's real name is Elon Musk.

242. AYE – Cinderella is the most popular fairy-tale of all time. 1) Cinderella, 2) Beauty and the Beast, 3) Little Red Riding Hood, 4) Snow White, 5) Jack and the Beanstalk.

243. AYE – Spider-Man is the current No. 1 superhero. 1) Spider-Man, 2) Wonder Woman, 3) Batman, 4) Ironman, 5) Superman.

244. NAW – Boxing burns more calories than tap-dancing, although it is close. Boxing – 800 calories, tap-dancing – 750 calories.

245. NAW – There are currently fourteen astronauts in space on three different space stations. This is a new record.

246. NAW – Bono formed a band at school and started gigging professionally at sixteen years old.

247. AYE – Even though 3.5 billion eat rice daily, more eat pizza! 1) Pizza, 2) Chinese, 3) Japanese cuisine. 84% believe Italian cuisine is the best.

248. NAW – There are more mice than pigeons. There are 400 million pigeons and 20 BILLION mice.

249. NAW – There are more dogs than cats. There are 400 million cats and 900 million dogs.

250. AYE – 70% of households in the UK own a BBQ. I don't. Make me a sausage, will you?

251. AYE – Peanuts are not nuts. They are legumes, same family as peas and lentils.

252. AYE – On this date, Spanish teams had won 213, England 173, Italy 162 and Germany 149.

253. AYE – There are more accountants than doctors. The UK has 380,000 accountants and 300,000 doctors.

254. AYE – Pepperoni sells the most in the UK, but worldwide plain old cheese is the top-selling pizza.

255. NAW – Turtles do not have teeth. They have beaks and very strong jaw muscles to crush food.

256. NAW – Oasis star Noel Gallagher is only five years older than brother Liam.

257. NAW – Red wine is marginally more popular than white in Scotland. 1) Red wine – 47%, 2) white wine – 42%, 2) rosé wine – 11%. I don't think Buckfast was included in this research.

258. NAW – Surprisingly more people live in London than the city of New York. London has 9.5 million, New York has 8.1 million and has a declining population.

259. NAW – Only 59% of people in the UK wear glasses or contact lenses.

260. AYE – Green is the second most common eye colour in the UK. 1) Blue – 48%, 2) green – 30%, 3) brown – 22%. Scotland and Ireland have more green eyes than any other countries in the world.

261. AYE – Primary school children in Armenia are all taught chess.

262. NAW – A single bee will only produce one-twelfth of a teaspoon of honey in its lifetime. It takes 1,152 bees 22,700 trips to make one jar of honey.

263. AYE – Over 80% of birds will not have male dangly bits! Chickens don't have them at all while ducks have big ones. That's quackers!

264. AYE – There are over 12,000 species of ant.

265. NAW – Adam Ant was born Stuart Leslie Godard in London. (Ant-igua . . . see what I did there?)

266. AYE – 'Stand and Deliver' was number 1 for five weeks in 1981; 'Ant Music', released in 1980, only got to number 2.

267. NAW – In *The Wizard of Oz* Dorothy lived with her Aunty Em.

268. NAW – Dec is older than Ant by two months.

269. NAW – There are currently 101 McDonald's and 100 Starbucks. (This may have changed now, but at time of question it was correct.)

270. AYE – Experts believe the Callanish Standing Stones were build 2900 BC, Stonehenge 2500 BC.

271. AYE – Eagles can sometimes eat baby monkeys and chimpanzees.

272. NAW – There will be an estimated 6,000 animals at the Royal Highland Show over four days.

273. NAW – A wild cheetah can run at 70mph, a greyhound can run at 45mph. However, the greyhound would beat a captive cheetah, whose top speed is 39mph.

274. AYE – More people play bingo than football. Bingo – 1.6 billion, football – 265 million.

275. AYE – Tennis is the most popular individual sport. 1) Tennis – 60 million players, 2) golf – 25 million.

276. AYE – Some fish can walk, including the snakehead fish, the cave angelfish and the spotted climbing perch. The latter can gulp air, store oxygen and use its pectoral fins as feet to walk to new pools of water.

277. NAW – Facebook has more monthly users than YouTube. 1) Facebook – 2.85 billion, 2) YouTube – 2.2 billion, 3) WhatsApp – 1.6 billion, 4) Instagram – 1 billion, 5) TikTok – 1 billion.

JULY – SEP 22

278. AYE – Beavers have orange teeth. They have long incisors that get their orange colour from an iron-rich protective coating of enamel. They grow continuously so must be used daily to keep them trim.

279. AYE – *Alice in Wonderland* is based on real life. Lewis Carroll wrote about his friend's daughter Alice Liddell. Her dad was so busy working, he was always rushing about and became his inspiration for the white rabbit.

280. AYE – Cows can only dream when they lie down. They can sleep standing up, but they never reach REM sleep, the stage where dreams occur. What do you think they dream about?

281. AYE – White chocolate is not chocolate as it does not contain any cocoa.

282. NAW – Kebabs originated in Turkey, where soldiers grilled chunks of wild animals on fires as early as 1377.

283. NAW – Mojitos were invented in Havana, Cuba. Made from rum, lime, sugar, fresh mint, crushed ice and club soda.

284. NAW – A cow has thirty-two teeth but none at the top front. They also chew forty to fifty times a minute.

285. NAW – French fries originated in Belgium, widely believed to have been invented by American soldiers based in Wallonia, where French is spoken, in WW1.

286. AYE – According to the letter of the law it is NOT an offence to be naked in public. However, and please take this seriously before being done for getting fully scuddy down your local, you can be arrested if it can be proven you deliberately stripped with the intent to shock or upset. Go on, give it a go …

287. AYE – Horses only breathe through their nostrils. They are nasal breathers. A structure called the soft palate completely separates the upper part of the airway above the mouth.

288. AYE – Only 3% of homes in the UK have air conditioning. 91% of homes in the US have it.

289. AYE – The daquiri was invented in the town of Daquiri in southeastern Cuba. An American engineer had a cocktail party and ran out of gin for the punch so used local rum instead. A basic daquiri is rum, lime juice, sugar syrup, and fruit.

290. NAW – The name 'lollipop' came from a racehorse called Lolly Pop. George Smith from Connecticut started making candy on sticks in 1908 and finally trademarked the name in 1931.

291. NAW – The average person will eat more burgers than pizzas in their lifetime. They will eat 970 burgers and 'only' 731 pizzas.

292. NAW – The mango is the national fruit of three countries: India, Pakistan and the Philippines. In case you wondered, the national fruit of Scotland is the apple.

293. NAW – Best place to go drinking in the UK is Blackpool. Glasgow was 35th. I demand a recount.

294. AYE – Almonds are the most consumed nut in the world: over 1.18 metric tonnes a year are scoffed. Over 42 million metric tonnes of peanuts are eaten each year, but they are technically a legume and not a nut as they grow underground.

295. NAW – Italy produces more white wine than any other country. 1) Italy – 44.5 million hectolitres, 2) Spain – 35 million hectolitres and 3) France – 34 hectolitres.

296. NAW – A cat would beat Usain Bolt over 100m. Cats can run at 30mph, Usain Bolt at his fastest could run 27.33mph.

297. AYE – The Eiffel Tower can be at least 15cm taller in the summer due to thermal expansion, which heats up the steel. Particles gain kinetic energy and take up more space.

298. AYE – All lion cubs are born with spots. Incidentally, why do lions eat raw meat? They cannae cook ☺.

299. AYE – More people live in Edinburgh (548,000) than Iceland (376,000)

300. AYE – Lightning is FIVE times hotter than the sun.

301. NAW – The first rollercoaster was in Paris around 200 years ago. A French builder brought 'Russian Mountains' to Paris, sledges on ice. However, Paris was too hot for this attraction, so he made wooden rails for the sledges.

302. NAW – There are 26 bones in each foot; 26 bones, 33 joints, 19 muscles, 10 tendons and 107 ligaments if you want to show off!

303. NAW – Jon Bon Jovi is not related to Dean Martin, but he IS related to Frank Sinatra. Frank was his father's great-uncle.

304. AYE – China grows the most potatoes in the world annually. 1) China – 80 million metric tonnes, 2) India – 51 million metric tonnes, 3) Ukraine – 20 million metric tonnes. The UK grows 5.5 million metric tonnes.

305. AYE – In *Toy Story* Buzz Lightyear was originally called 'Lunar Larry'.

306. NAW – *Titanic* was the highest grossing film of the nineties raking in £660 million, *Jurassic Park* was second with £450 million.

307. NAW – Beyoncé is not godmother to Moses Martin, but her ex-husband, Jay-Z, is his godfather.

308. NAW – Coldplay were not in the Top 5 highest earning touring bands in 2022, they're ninth. Bad Bunny – £120 million, 2) Genesis – £72 million, 3) Elton John – £70 million.

309. AYE – Only 30% of the population uses toilet roll. Large areas of southern Europe, Africa and Asia use water instead.

310. AYE – The world high jump record is 8ft 1.4in which is 2.45m. Which is nearly two full Jimmy Krankies set in 1993 by Cuban Javier Sotomayor.

311. AYE – The ginger gene is on the X chromosome. Females have XX so both need to be ginger, males are XY so only one needs to be ginger, therefore more males.

312. AYE – High levels of salt and sugar means coconut water can be used as a plasma substitute in emergencies. It was widely used in WW2.

313. AYE – Freddie Mercury was a champion boxer, a talented sprinter and a school table tennis champion.

314. NAW – Seagulls are monogamous and generally stick to one life partner.

315. NAW – Salami does come from the Latin word 'salare' but this means to add salt.

316. NAW – There are 852 episodes of *Star Trek* and 870 episodes of *Dr Who*.

317. NAW – Minecraft is the highest selling video game of all time. Grand Theft Auto is second. Minecraft has sold 238 million copies. Grand Theft Auto and Tetris are the only other games to sell over 1 million.

318. AYE – Dairy Milk is the UK's bestselling chocolate bar. 1) Dairy Milk, 2) Galaxy, 3) Lindt Lindor, 4) Maltesers, 5) KitKat.

319. NAW – The average man in the UK has NINE pairs of shoes.

320. NAW – 40 million baseball caps are sold worldwide each year in an industry worth $18 Billion. 80% are sold in the USA.

321. NAW – Guacamole translates from Aztec as avocado sauce. Ahuaca = avocado, mole = sauce.

322. AYE – The Giant Squid has the largest eyes in the world at 27cm, the size of a large football.

323. AYE – The origins of mini golf can be traced back to St Andrews in 1827, initially a small putting course created for lady golfers. It became popular in the US in the 1900s when the 'Thistle Do' course added windmills, tunnels and fun obstacles. In the 1920s many skyscrapers in New York had mini golf courses on their rooftops.

324. AYE – Elephants can NOT jump. They are widely believed to be the only mammal that is unable to jump because their legs, knees and ankles are not strong enough to leap and land safely.

325. AYE – There are 282 Munros in Scotland.

326. NAW – The top speed an alpaca can reach is 35mph.

327. AYE – The first milkshake recorded in print was in 1887; it was made from milk, eggs and whisky. 1922 in Chicago was when the milkshake made with ice cream and strawberry or chocolate syrup became popular.

328. NAW – The most googled question is 'What is my IP?' with 3.3 million monthly searches. 'What is the time?' is second with 1.8 million monthly searches. 'How do I vote?' and 'How do I tie a tie?' are the third and fourth most asked questions.

329. NAW – We still drink more tea than coffee in the UK: 100 million cups of tea every day compared to 95 million cups of coffee, although the gap is narrowing.

330. AYE – There are ten. Arm, ear, eye, gum, hip, jaw, leg, lip, rib and toe.

OCT – DEC 22

331. NAW – Koala's have fingerprints most like humans. Scientists claim they could compromise a crime scene!

332. AYE – A litre of water weighs more than a litre of vodka. Alcohol is less dense. A litre of vodka weighs 789 grams, a litre of water ways 1000 grams (1kg).

333. AYE – Bananas are radioactive. They are full of potassium and a small fraction of all potassium is radioactive. Each banana emits 0.1 millirems of radioactivity, meaning you would have to eat at least 10 MILLION bananas to be in danger.

334. AYE – More instant noodles are eaten in India. In India there are 6.8 billion servings of noodles a year, in Japan the figure is 5.7 billion.

335. NAW – Bert and Ernie were named after characters in the film *It's a Wonderful Life*. Bert was the policeman; Ernie drove the local cab.

336. AYE – The Manhattant is a species of ant first discovered by biologists between 63rd and 76th street in New York. It's a reddish brown ant with a brown head and contains more carbon than other ants thought to be from its diet of corn syrup prevalent in fast food.

337. NAW – A sloth can only poop a third of its body weight. They only go once a week so this must still feel momentous!

338. AYE – Saying 'prunes' puckers the lips for a more serious demeanour.

339. AYE – There are more trees than stars. According to NASA, there are 400 billion stars in the Milky Way galaxy and more than 3 trillion trees on Earth.

340. NAW – The biggest pyramid is in Mexico. The pyramid Cholula, Puebla is four times the size of the Great Pyramid of Giza. Although it is now partially buried under a mountain.

341. NAW – The UK Halloween market in 2022 is worth £687 million. That's a lot of monkey nuts!

342. AYE – Robbie Williams was a double-glazing salesman until his mum spotted an advert for a boy band audition in their local paper.

343. NAW – The monster in *Frankenstein* never had a name.

344. NAW – Argyll is the spookiest place according to PsychicWorld with more people claiming to have seen a ghost in that area than anywhere else in the UK, with over one hundred reported sightings per year.

345. NAW – Calzone pizzas were invented in Naples, Italy.

346. NAW – Scientist reckon 51–80% of oxygen is produced from algae in the seas and oceans.

347. AYE – Since the nineties scientists have been researching the effects of weightlessness on the development of jellyfish they've sent to space. In one experiment they sent 20,000 jellyfish polyps and returned with 60,000. However, space jellyfish struggle to swim when they return to Earth and suffer vertigo.

348. AYE – Gravy is the most important ingredient in a roast dinner. 1) Gravy, 2) roast potatoes, 3) meat, 4) Yorkshire puddings, 5) carrots.

349. NAW – Mick Jagger is a year older than Keith Richards.

350. AYE – Liza Thomas from Australia made 420 cappuccinos in one hour in December 2018.

351. AYE – The UK's favourite pudding in 2022 is sticky toffee pudding. 1) Sticky toffee pudding, 2) chocolate cake, 3) apple crumble, 4) profiteroles, 5) chocolate mousse.

352. AYE – Bert has a twin called Bart, who is always super cheery.

353. AYE – Cleopatra, Queen of Egypt, ate pickles because she thought they helped keep her beautiful. Caesar gave them to his troops to keep them strong.

354. NAW – The Beatles have had more No. 1's than Westlife. The Beatles have 17, Westlife have 14.

355. NAW – Dave Grohl dropped out of school aged seventeen to tour with a rock band called Scream and didn't even start university.

356. AYE – Gloria Estefan plays clarinet, has a psychology degree, is fluent in English, French and Spanish and was once head-hunted by the CIA.

357. AYE – Australia is wider than the moon by about 600km. The diameter of Australia from east to west is 4000km, the diameter of the moon is 3400km.

358. NAW – Mickey Mouse and Minnie Mouse celebrate their birthday on the same day, both were created on 18 November 1928.

359. AYE – Westlife have more than double the number of No. 1's than Boyzone. Westlife have 14 No. 1's, Boyzone have 6.

360. AYE – The A1 is the longest numbered road in the UK. It is 396 miles long running from Edinburgh to London.

361. NAW – 'No Matter What' was Boyzone's biggest selling song, shifting over 4 million copies.

362. NAW – The Backstreet Boys are the biggest selling boyband of all time. They have sold over 130 million albums, Take That have sold around 45 million.

363. AYE – Brazil is the largest country in South America. 1) Brazil – 3.2m square miles, 2) Argentina – 1m square miles, 3) Peru – 494,000 square miles.

364. NAW – Rod Stewart's dad was born in Leith, Edinburgh.

365. NAW – There are only five miles of fairy lights on the Rockefeller tree, containing 50,000 LED lights.

366. AYE – The population of Morocco is 37.3 million. The population of Portugal is 10.3 million; Switzerland, 8.6m. Portugal plus Switzerland is 18.9 million, still considerably less than Morocco.

367. NAW – Google was originally called 'Backrub'.

368. AYE – Dogs can be left-pawed or right-pawed, they have a preference relating to the stronger hemisphere in their brain.

369. AYE – Three Scottish footballers have been placed in FIFA's Player of the Year or Ballon D'or. In 1964 Dennis Law from Man Utd won Gold, in 1967 Jimmy Johnstone with Celtic was awarded Bronze and in 1983 Liverpool's Kenny Dalglish won Silver.

370. AYE – The snow on Venus is metal. On top of the mountains there is a layer of snow but given that the planet is so hot, snow as we know it can't exist. Instead, the mountains are topped by two types of metal: galena and bismuthinite. The rain on Venus is extremely corrosive sulphuric acid.

371. NAW – Argentina with a population of 46.2 million has 11.5 times the population of Croatia.

372. NAW – The current capital of Morocco is Rabat. There are four imperial cities: Marrakesh, Rabat, Fez and Meknes but Rabat is the official capital.

373. AYE – The small intestine is narrower and longer, generally 9–16ft, while the large intestine usually measures 5ft.

374. AYE – Blue is one of the three primary colours along with red and yellow.

375. AYE – Only male turkeys can make the 'gobble-gobble' noise. It is a unique call to attract females during breeding season. Female turkeys can only chirp and cluck!

376. AYE – 21 December was the winter solstice in 2022.

377. NAW – Apricot trees can produce fruit for twenty to twenty-five years max.

378. AYE – Frogs can be hypnotised if you lay them on their backs and rub their tummies (although I've never tried this). Lizards, chickens and alligators are also susceptible to hypnosis. Although good luck trying to convince an alligator he is a racehorse.

379. NAW – Switzerland is bordered by FIVE countries. France, Italy, Germany, Austria and Lichtenstein.

380. AYE – 140 million people in the world are gingers, which is roughly 2%. Scotland has the highest percentage per population at 13% followed by Ireland at 10%.

381. AYE – According to the Oxford English Dictionary the letter 'e' appears in 11% of all words.

382. AYE – Canada has 243,042km of coastline, including islands. Top 5 is 1) Canada, 2) Indonesia – 54,716km, 3) Russia – 37,653km, 4) USA – 19,924km, 5) China – 14,500km.

383. NAW – Popeye first appeared on 17 January 1929. So, it was the 1920s.

384. AYE – Winnie the Pooh was based on a real life female Canadian black bear called Winnie who lived in London Zoo between 1920–1930s. A.A. Milne's son Christopher Robin had a teddy bear and called him Winnie, and thus the stories and adventures began.

385. NAW – Halloumi is the FOURTH most popular cheese in the UK. 1) Cheddar, 2) red Leicester, 3) mozzarella, 4) halloumi, 5) Brie.

386. NAW – Grolsch Lager is brewed in the Netherlands and shoes still look silly with the tops on them!

387. NAW – Chicken and mushroom is the most popular savoury pie in the UK. 1) Chicken and mushroom, 2) steak pie, 3) cheese and onion, 4) shepherd's pie. Personally, I think a macaroni pie covered in brown sauce should be topping that list.

388. AYE – Over a million Coca-Cola bottles were produced in 2009 with Rabbie Burns' face on them to commemorate the year of Homecoming Scotland.

389. AYE – Andy Bell once sold shoes in Dogsthorpe, Peterborough back in 1985.

390. AYE – Chocolate cake is the third most popular cake in the UK. 1) Banana bread (not happy with that answer, what kind of cake is that? It is in the name BREAD, NOT CAKE, anyway, the official survey says this, so I'll have to go with it), 2) Victoria sponge, 3) chocolate cake, 4) red velvet cake, 5) sticky toffee pudding.

391. AYE – Bubble wrap was invented in New Jersey in 1957 by engineers Alfred Feilding and Marc Chavannes to be used as wallpaper. It didn't do well, so they repurposed it as greenhouse insulation, eventually moving on to protective wrapping.

392. NAW – His real name IS Justin Randall Timberlake.

393. AYE – The most popular password IS 123456. Top 4 are 1) 12345, 2) 1234567, 3) QWERTY, 4) Password.

394. NAW – 'Jambos' was derived from the nickname the Jam Tarts. This came from soldiers returning from WW1 who had shared the trenches with Cockney Soldiers. With Cockney rhyming slang, Hearts became the Jam Tarts, which over time became Jambos.

395. NAW – There are 14,820 dachshunds and only 11,808 golden retrievers. Labradors are the most popular breed with 61,559 in the UK.

396. NAW – Only 33% of the 7.88 billion people in the world use chopsticks on a daily basis.

397. AYE – Ballet first appeared in the Italian Renaissance courts around 1500. When Catherine de' Medici married

Henry II of France, SHE introduced it to the French courts. Ballet is originally Italian.

398. NAW – Kites were first flown in China around 1000BC.

399. NAW – Fry's Chocolate Cream is the longest running chocolate bar still sold today. It was first produced in 1866. Bournville chocolate was first introduced in 1879, with Cadbury's Dairy Milk appearing in 1905.

400. AYE – Too ******* right we do. Glaswegians swear more than anywhere else in the UK: 15.2 per 100 words posted on social media by Glaswegians are deemed swear words. 1) Glasgow, 2) Liverpool – they have 8.7 per 100, 3) London – 8.5 per 100, 4) Edinburgh – 8.4 per 100.

401. NAW – Mardi Gras means 'Fat Tuesday'. Always falls the Tuesday before Ash Wednesday where traditionally rich fatty foods are eaten ahead of the start of Lent.

402. NAW – Drew Barrymore's second highest grossing film was *Batman Forever*. 1) *E.T*, – $792m, 2) *Batman Forever* – $336m, 3) *Charlie's Angels* – $259m.

403. AYE – Eggs are the UK's favourite toast topping. 1) Eggs, 2) butter, 3) jam, 4) marmalade, 5) cheese.

404. AYE – Starfish do NOT have brains. They do not have any blood either.

405. AYE – There are NO polar bears in Antarctica. They all live in Northern Arctic regions.

406. AYE – The most popular colour of car in the UK in 2023 is grey. 1) Grey – 24.8%, 2) black – 20.5%, 3) white – 17%.

407. NAW – Sharks are unable to sneeze. They have two nostrils, but they don't join the back of their throat like ours. To get debris out of their nostrils they must shake their heads.

408. NAW – In 2022 FOUR times as many books were sold than eBooks. Only 18% of all books sold were eBooks.

409. NAW – Tom Cruise is one year younger than George Clooney. Cruise is sixty, Clooney is sixty-one. Don't they look fine? ☺

410. AYE – Andy Murray has played in eleven Grand Slam Finals and won three. Wimbledon in 2013 and 2016 and the US Open in 2012.

411. NAW – 59% of children in the UK aged ten or under have mobile phones.

412. NAW – Ursula von der Leyen is the most powerful woman in the world, she is President of the European Commission. Kamala Harris, the US Vice President, is third in the list after Christine Lagarde, the French politician who is President of the European Central Bank.

413. AYE – The plural of the same kind of fish is fish. The plural of different species of fish is fishes.

414. NAW – Amsterdam has more canals than Venice. Amsterdam has 160 canals, Venice has 150.

415. AYE – Central Park, New York according to Instagram is the most popular place in the world to get engaged. 1) Central Park, New York, 2) Eiffel Tower, Paris, 3) Brooklyn Bridge, New York, 4) The Grand Canyon, 5) Santorini, Greece.

416. AYE – Barack Obama is the most followed person on Twitter. On this day the rankings were: 1) Obama 133m, 2) Elon Musk 130m, 3) Justin Bieber 113.5m, 4) Katy Perry 108.6m, 5) Rhianna 108.3 m. (Although chances are Musk will now be first.)

417. NAW – Seals can sleep at depth under the water by holding their breath and also by bobbing in the water horizontally with their noses pointing to the sky.

418. AYE – A jiffy is a unit of time. A jiffy is one-hundredth of a second. People who tell you they will 'be there in a jiffy' are most probably talking mince.

419. AYE – Scotland have played Cyprus seven times so far and won all seven matches.

420. AYE – Scotland have collectively won and drawn more games v Spain than they have lost. (Wins 3 + draws 4 = 7, Spain have won 6.) Remember, this is the answer to the question on this date.

421. AYE – The Eiffel Tower is over 30m higher than when it first opened: there have been sections added and a massive DAB radio mast attached to the top.

APRIL – JUNE 23

422. NAW – The 'L' in Samuel L Jackson is for Leroy.

423. AYE – Rats will giggle if tickled, although the pitch is too high for humans to hear. Researchers say they emit high-pitched tiny giggles when tickled and show positive emotion when tickled. Belly tickles work best!

424. AYE – Transport Scotland maintain 2,029 road bridges in Scotland.

425. NAW – The most popular tartan remains the Royal Stewart, the bright red one featured on most souvenirs.

426. AYE – Patrick Wills from Virginia carded THREE 'hole in ones' in one round playing in an amateur tournament at Laurel Hill Golf Club, Virginia. He finished with a 14 under par 57.

427. AYE – 7% of Americans believe chocolate milk comes from brown cows, that is 16.4 million people.

428. AYE – To date there are 1,308 episodes of *River City* in 24 seasons. Dallas has 357 episodes in 14 seasons, *Dynasty* has 108 episodes in 5 seasons, *Knots Landing* has 344 episodes in 14 series. Add them together and they have 809 episodes, still way below the *River City* count.

429. AYE – Volkswagen make more sausages than cars. They make and sell over 9 million sausages a year and 8.2 million cars. VW have made currywurst sausages since 1973 at their Wolfsburg factory. Originally manufactured for workers, they now supply supermarkets and football stadiums in Germany.

430. AYE – There is only one ten-point letter, 'Z', in scrabble, so the other would have to be a zero-point blank tile. Therefore, QUIZ would score twenty-two points, while JAZZ would only score nineteen points.

431. NAW – Only three grey horses have won the Grand National, although they have won four Nationals as The Lamb won in 1867 AND 1868. The other grey winners were Nicolaus Silver in 1961 and Neptune Collonges in 2012.

432. NAW – Wombats poop perfect squares. They are the only animal in the world able to poop cuboids. They poop nearly 100 a day and use them to mark their territory. The square shape makes them more difficult to roll away. Ouch!

433. NAW – White blood cells are on average three times bigger than red blood cells. However, there are 600 red blood cells for every one white one. Red cells carry oxygen, white cells fight infection.

434. NAW – Canada is the second biggest country in the world. 1) Russia, 2) Canada, 3) China, 4) USA. I'm sure I've already told you this! ☺

435. NAW – In Greek mythology Diana is the goddess of hunting. Aphrodite is the goddess of love.

436. NAW – The Battle of Bannockburn took place in 1314. The Declaration of Arbroath was 1320!

437. AYE – It can rain diamonds on Uranus and Neptune. Diamond rain forms when hydrogen and carbon are squeezed together by high pressure. This causes solid diamonds to form, which can sink further into the planet's interior like rain.

438. NAW – Band Aid 'Do They Know It's Christmas?' was the biggest selling single of the 1980s. 1) Band Aid – 'Do They Know It's Christmas?', 2) Frankie Goes to Hollywood – 'Relax', 3) Wham – 'Last Christmas'.

439. NAW – To date, 6,098 people have reached the summit of Everest, while 622 people from 44 countries have reached space.

440. NAW – *Brothers in Arms* by Dire Straits was the top-selling album of the 1980s. 1) Dire Straits – *Brothers in Arms*, 2) Michael Jackson – *Bad*, 3) Michael Jackson – *Thriller*, 4) Queen – *Greatest Hits*, 5) Kylie Minogue – *Kylie*.

441. AYE – The bestselling album of the nineties was Oasis with *(What's the Story) Morning Glory?* selling 4.9 million (now 22 million) copies. 1) Oasis – *(What's the Story) Morning Glory?*, 2) Simply Red – *Stars*, 3) Spice Girls – *Spice*, 4) The Corrs – *Talk on Corners*, 5) Alanis Morissette – *Jagged Little Pill*.

442. NAW – Simon and Garfunkel's album *Bridge Over Troubled Water* was the bestselling album of the 1970s. 1) Simon and Garfunkel – *Bridge Over Troubled Water*, 2) ABBA – *Greatest Hits*, 3) Mike Oldfield – Tubular Bells, 4) Simon and Garfunkel – *Greatest Hits*, 5) Various – *Saturday Night Fever – Original Soundtrack*.

443. AYE – There are six white stripes of the zebra crossing visible on the *Abbey Road* cover.

444. AYE – *Star Wars* sound engineer Ben Burtt used the sounds of a badger, lion, seal and walrus to create Chewbacca's distinctive voice.

445. NAW – Ireland have won the most Eurovision Song Contest titles with seven. Sweden is second having won six. Luxenberg, The Netherlands and the UK each have five victories.

446. AYE – There have been five barefoot winners. 1) Sandy Shaw in 1967, 2) Serteb Erner in 2003, 3) Dima Belan in 2008, 4) Loreen in 2012 and 5) Emmelie de Forest in 2013.

447. NAW – Norway is the country who have finished last the most in Eurovision. They have placed bottom on eleven occasions.

448. NAW – Mae Muller was not in a Kylie video. She was, however, in Mika's video for the song 'Grace Kelly'.

449. NAW – A 'Swedish kiss' is a quick close-mouthed kiss that we would call a peck. No noses were slobbered on researching this question!

450. NAW – The first engine powered double decker bus was unveiled in London in 1926. It was, however, based on an idea first seen in Paris – the horse drawn double decker omnibus.

451. NAW – There are more bathrooms in Buckingham Palace. Buckingham Palace has seventy-eight bathrooms; the White House has thirty-five.

452. AYE – Herbie is famously 53, the General Lee is 01. Add them together you get 54, which is less than 60.

453. NAW – Beyoncé's real name IS Beyoncé Gisele Knowles.

454. AYE – Before he was confirmed Sherlock Holmes, Arthur Conan Doyle named his detective 'Sherrinford Hope'.

455. NAW – There were 37 more episodes of *Cheers*. *Friends* – 236 episodes v *Cheers* – 273 episodes.

456. NAW – There are 84,600 seconds in a day, which is less than 90,000.

457. AYE – The Tina Turner Highway is a section of the Tennessee state route 19 which runs through Nutbush, the town where she was born.

458. NAW – The first marathon was run in Greece. Legend has it Pheidippides, a courier for the court, ran from Marathon to Athens with battle news. The distance was 26.3 miles.

459. NAW – Ladybirds are both male and female. Sometimes the male ladybird is known as a gentlemen ladybird. They are generally smaller than the females.

460. NAW – 74% of people in the UK wear glasses or have had corrective surgery.

461. NAW – *The Lion King* has sold the most VHS copies with over 30 million sales. 1) *The Lion King,* 2) *Aladdin,* 3) *Snow White,* 4) *Titanic.*

462. NAW – Slugs have more teeth than sharks. Slugs can have 27,000 microscopic teeth on a flexible band near their jaws called their radula. Sharks can have 50–300 teeth in several rows.

463. NAW – Metallica are the only band to have played on every continent. They did a tour in 2013 which included gigs in all seven continents and by doing so got themselves into the *Guinness Book of Records*. They played a small gig on Antarctica for scientists!

464. AYE – Superman's real human name is Clark Joseph Kent. He was known as 'Kal–el' when he was on the planet Krypton.

465. AYE – There are nearly 400 flavours of KitKat in Japan. They are known as 'Kitto Katto', which sounds like 'Kitto Katsu' and means good luck. People give KitKats for luck! Unusual flavours include red bean, baked potato, green tea, apple and butter.

466. NAW – Sir Tom Jones did tell a reporter he got chocolate sent to him from the UK, but it was After Eights, NOT Terry's Chocolate Orange.

467. AYE – Gambas al ajillo is the most popular tapas dish in the world. 1) Gambas al ajillo, 2) patatas bravas, 3) calamari, 4) chorizo vino tinto, 5) jamon iberico.

468. NAW – There are over thirty Aberdeens in the world as you learned earlier in this book; none of them are in Norway.

469. NAW – Kenny McLean never played squash for Scotland. He did, however, squash Norway with that very late goal. ☺

470. NAW – Georgia the state has a much higher population than Georgia the country: 10.8 million for the state and 3.7 million for the country.

471. NAW – It 'only' lasted 3 hours and 23 mins. Stockport v Doncaster in 1946. Finished 2–2 after extra time and was part of a trial tournament which implemented a 'play to the finish' rule. Like a golden goal but with no time limit. It ended up getting too dark and getting replayed. Doncaster won.

472. NAW – There will be competitors from over thirty countries, but not quite fifty countries, taking part in the sheep shearing competition at the Royal Highland Show.

473. AYE – Charlie is the guitar-playing Proclaimer. Craig plays harmonica and the tambourine, and both share the vocals.

474. NAW – Elton John's piano was a custom-built Yamaha Disklavia, but it 'only' cost £1.3 million.

475. AYE – 'Knocking on Heaven's Door' was the highest placed single from Guns N' Roses in the UK charts reaching No. 2 in 1990.

476. AYE – Jenny and Carol were both on the show for five years each, but Jenny presented more episodes.

477. NAW – According to Steve Jobs, the 'I' in iPhone stands for 'internet, individual, instruct, inform and inspire'.

478. NAW – A porcupine would beat a hedgehog over 20m. Porcupines run at 6mph while hedgehogs can only manage 4mph.

GREATEST HITS RADIO

479. AYE – Fred has a certificate in potato rogueing from Elmwood College in Cupar, Fife.

480. NAW – Ken trained as an accountant and then washed cars for a living before embarking on his radio career.

481. NAW – Ewen ran semi-naked around Ibrox but it was a bet about Rangers signing Jean-Alain Boumsong not Dado Prso.

482. AYE – Jackie appeared in *Four Weddings and a Funeral* as a guest at the first wedding.

483. NAW – Webster has never owned a pet snake!

484. AYE – Boogie had a massive crush on Emma Bunton AKA Baby Spice and did ask her out. She didn't say no, but she didn't say yes either. Bless.

485. AYE – Arlene once got her head shaved when she was seven after her brother chopped lumps out of it with blunt kitchen scissors and shaving was considered the only option.

486. NAW – To date, Andy has never needed to be rescued by hotel staff from a bog!

487. AYE – Fred flew a Tornado over Scotland as a thank you from RAF Lossiemouth for speaking at their Burns Supper. Ewen McGregor's brother Colin was the pilot and he let Fred take control for a few seconds.

488. AYE – Ken has a collection of seven vintage buses, including his very own double decker.

489. AYE – Ewen unsuccessfully tried to pull Clare Balding in Dubai. Turns out he just wasn't her type!

490. AYE – Jackie was initially of interest to the CIA as a trained journalist prepared to learn Farsi, but she did not progress as she was not a US citizen.

491. AYE – Webster won a piggyback race on the back of Tom Stoltman, who was the world's strongest man at the time. It took place at the Blairgowrie Highland Games in 2019.

492. AYE – Boogie sang ACDC 'Highway to Hell' with a band at his wedding . . . and she still said yes!

493. NAW – Even though Arlene is an excellent speller, she never won a school competition for spelling 'diarrhoea' correctly.

494. AYE – Andy Crane was on *EastEnders*. Well, they showed him presenting on a telly in a living room in one episode, so he is claiming it.

495. NAW – Fred enjoys a dook in his local pool but has never attempted a River Tay crossing.

496. AYE – Ken plays drums in No Direction. They gig in bars and clubs in Oxfordshire.

497. NAW – Thankfully Ewen has never been a swimwear model, so please do NOT encourage him.

498. NAW – Jackie and Britney are both bubbly beautiful blondes but there is no other connection.

499. AYE – Webster has tiny non-pierceable nipples! He tried. The piercer said no.

500. AYE – Arlene dipped her boob in tomato soup in front of her future in-laws the first time they met. She was also wearing a cream top and was trying to shuffle along a table to get to another seat when it happened. Nobody said a word. It felt nice.

Conclusion

There you go. *Ewen and Cat's Wee Book of Aye or Naw?* is over. FIVE HUNDRED 'Aye or Naw' questions completed. I hope you've enjoyed them and had some fun along the way. You'll no doubt have learned some remarkable facts to make you a much more interesting person down the pub and you'll probably have argued with pals over some of the more ridiculous questions.

As I mentioned at the start of this book, at the time of going to print ALL of these answers were correct. Some might change over time, a few might be disputed by boffins, but to the best of my knowledge and online research they should be right.

Feel free to buy lots of extra copies of this book for everyone at your work, all your neighbours, your pals and your family. You will be educating them and also doing a very good thing to help support families and children in Scotland who are struggling right now.

On behalf of Ewen and I, everyone at Greatest Hits Radio and Cash for Kids, THANK YOU!

Cat xx

Is this the end? **AYE!**

FOR NOW ...

Thank You

To all my friends and family, thanks for everything. I need my pals like 3 a.m. chips need cheese.

To the Milngavie girls, my West End girls, all my panto/theatre pals, Marcia, neighbour Rod and Stuarty, thanks for keeping me sane. Debbie, Joe and Mrs P, thanks for the grub!

Ewen, you always have my back, and I will always have yours. I am very proud of you – and you know why.

To my immediate radio gang: Wee Vixen, Producer Michael, and Producer Cat, you're all absolutely mental and that is why it works. Never change!

Producer Carnage, Producer Roo-ray, Producer Chris and Producer Finn have all stepped in to play 'Aye or Naw' at some point and generally whipped Ewen's sorry ass.

A special mention to panto legend Johnny Mac, who has pestered me relentlessly for two years to write an 'Aye or Naw' book so he can torment his lovely family on Christmas Day.

Thanks also to Kirsty and Ross MacGregor from Imagine Images for the cover photo, they are a joy to work with.

To Campbell Brown and everyone at Black and White Publishing for their ongoing support.

Also thank you to Grace Reilly and all the Cash for Kids team. What a job they do making life just that little bit easier for so many people in need.

My super talented niece Jessica Harvey has done an incredible job with the illustrations for this book whilst still at uni. I'll pay you in fizz and pizza just like I promised! ☺

To Paul McManus from Gun for all your support for my previous book for Cash for Kids, you really are a star! Also hello to my wee pal Ellis Easton-Riley, who is my favourite ghostbuster and wanted to be included as he wants to work on Ewen and Cat at Breakfast when he grows up!

To PR Guru Peter Samson and all the fabulous style team at Taylor Ferguson's, including Taylor, Anne, Mags, John, Tammy and Leeane, who make me presentable for charity hosting duties throughout the year, and to Bill and Sonia, my wonderful downstairs neighbours, for letting me borrow Sherlock, their incredible dog, whenever I need to switch off and relax.

And most of all, once again, thank you for buying this book and ultimately helping Cash for Kids navigate others through a very difficult time.

Is that me finally done? AYE!

Also available

In CAT'S OUT THE BAG, Cat spills the beans on the behind-the-scenes antics on one of Scotland's favourite radio shows. Side-splittingly funny, insightful, poignant and ultimately uplifting in a world of gloom, this is the banter we all need.

www.blackandwhitepublishing.com